HOW TO KNOW YOU

GW00738346

In this Series

How to Be an Effective School Governor
How to Buy & Run a Shop
How to Choose a Private School
How to Claim State Benefits
How to Do Your Own Advertising
How to Employ and Manage Staff
How to Enjoy Retirement
How to Get a Job Abroad
How to Get That Job
How to Help Your Child at School
How to Invest in Stocks & Shares
How to Keep Business Accounts
How to Know Your Rights at Work
How to Know Your Rights Over Sixty
How to Know Your Rights: Patients
How to Know Your Rights: Students
How to Know Your Rights: Teachers
How to Live & Work in America
How to Live & Work in Australia
How to Live & Work in Belgium
How to Live & Work in France
How to Live & Work in Germany
How to Live & Work in Saudi Arabia
How to Live & Work in Spain
How to Lose Weight & Keep Fit
How to Make It in Films and TV
How to Master Business English
How to Master Public Speaking
How to Pass Exams Without Anxiety
How to Pass That Interview
How to Plan a Wedding
How to Prepare Your Child for School
How to Raise Business Finance
How to Run a Local Campaign
How to Start a Business from Home
How to Study Abroad
How to Study & Live in Britain
How to Survive at College
How to Survive Divorce
How to Take Care of Your Heart
How to Teach Abroad
How to Use a Library
How to Write a Report
How to Write for Publication

KNOW YOUR
RIGHTS AT WORK

Robert Spicer

Barrister

How To Books

British Library Cataloguing-in-Publication Data
Spicer, Robert
   How to know your rights at work. – (How to books)
   I. Title   II. Series
   331.0942026

   ISBN 1–85703–009–5

Note
The material contained in this book is set out in good faith for general guidance and no liability can be accepted for loss or expense incurred as a result of relying in particular circumstances on statements made in the book. Readers are also reminded that laws and regulations are liable to change.

First published in 1991 by How To Books Ltd, Plymbridge House, Estover Road, Plymouth PL6 7PZ, United Kingdom. Tel: (0752) 705251. Fax: (0752) 695699.

Typeset by PDQ Typesetting, Stoke-on-Trent
Printed and bound in Great Britain by Dotesios Ltd, Trowbridge, Wiltshire

Contents

Preface

Whilst every care has been taken to ensure that the contents of this book are accurate and up-to-date, it is essential for readers to be aware that the law of employment is complex and rapidly-changing. This book aims to give a broad picture of the legal rights of employers and employees. It cannot be regarded as a substitute for professional advice in individual cases. Detailed legal advice on employment matters is available not only from professional lawyers but also from a wide range of sources including trade unions, employers' associations, Citizens Advice Bureaux, the Equal Opportunities Commission and the Commission for Racial Equality. Details of these organisations are given at the end of the book.

In general, the rules discussed in this book apply only to England and Wales. Every effort has been made to state the law as it stands in December 1990.

Some areas of employment law are so complex that they cannot be given justice in an introductory book like this. In these areas, real life cases have been inserted so as to show the reader the type of problems which courts and tribunals have to face, and how they go about resolving them.

Technical jargon has been kept to a minimum, but where such terms are unavoidable, they have been explained in the Glossary. The word 'he' has been used in places to stand for 'he or she'; no discrimination is intended or should be implied.

Robert Spicer

An Employee's Guide to the Legal System
Tribunals and Courts in England and Wales

The civil law

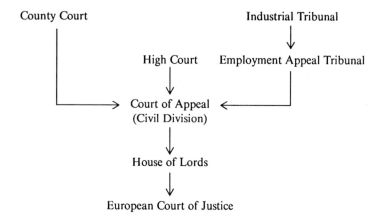

The criminal law

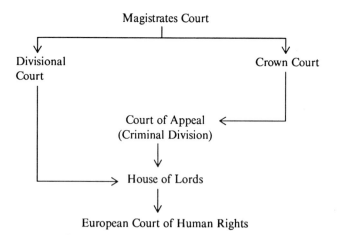

1
Your Legal Status
at Work

In order to appreciate what rights (and duties) you have as an employee, it is necessary to understand your legal status at work. As an employee you are entitled to a written statement of your terms of employment, and we will consider this in detail in the next chapter.

But your contract of employment is far from being the only thing which governs your legal status at work. The whole framework of English civil and criminal law has a bearing on it. In this chapter we will consider some of the key aspects of your legal status at work including:

- the legal framework of statute and common law (civil and criminal)
- rights and duties of employers and employees
- the scope of employment
- confidential information
- references
- being a company director

THE LEGAL FRAMEWORK

The origins of employment law
Laws governing employment have their roots a long way back in English history, and reflect a centuries-old process of social, political and economic change.

'Conspirators be they that do confer or bind themselves by Oath, Covenant or other Alliance, that every of them shall aid and support the Enterprise of each other falsely and maliciously to indite, or cause to be indited, or falsely to move or maintain pleas.'

This is an extract from the Third Ordinance of Conspirators issued as long ago as 1304; it is one of the earliest examples of an Act which was used in the field of employment. In this case its purpose was to bring charges of conspiracy against combining groups of workers.

The law of employment changes rapidly and has always been a political football. Legal rules in the employment field tend to come and go with changing governments. The first employment laws date from the Middle Ages, but modern statutes started to develop in the nineteenth century.

In Victorian times the subject was known as 'the law of Master and Servant'. Today we use the term employment law, or labour law, but traces of the old Victorian attitudes can still be found in some surviving laws.

English statute and common law
English law may be broadly divided into **statute** and **common law**.

- **Statutes** are Acts of Parliament, passed by both the House of Commons and the House of Lords, and signed by the Sovereign.

- **Common law** means the body of actual cases decided by the courts which explain that statutory material.

Thus, if anyone wishes to find out the law on a particular area of employment law, for example unfair dismissal, they must look first at the statute and then at the cases interpreting it.

There is also a distinction between **criminal** and **civil** law (see below) but both are governed by statute and common law.

Much employment law is now governed by statute. Detailed **statutory rights** have been created by Parliament, in particular in the areas of redundancy, contracts of employment, unfair dismissal, discrimination and health and safety.

Recent statutes
A modern example of a statute as an instrument of economic policy is the **Industrial Relations Act 1971**. This Act expressed the policy of the Labour government as set out in its 1969 document, *In Place of Strife*. The following extract, section 22(1) of that Act, shows a typical section of an Act of Parliament:

Unfair dismissal
Right of employee not to be unfairly dismissed
22(1) In every employment to which this section applies every employee shall have the right not to be unfairly dismissed by his employer...

Other examples of modern statutes are the **Equal Pay Act 1970**, the **Health and Safety at Work Act 1974**, and the **Wages Act 1986**, to name but three. A list of the most important ones appears at the end of this book.

Some statutes relate to the civil law (for example the laws of contract or property). Other statutes have the force of the criminal law behind them, since breach of their provisions can result in fines or imprisonment. For example, breach of the Health and Safety at Work Act is, as we will see in a later chapter, a matter for criminal prosecution.

Recent cases
Cases involving employment law are coming before the tribunals and courts all the time. Throughout this book we will use a selection of recent cases to try and illustrate how different questions have been dealt with in practice. As we will see, while statute law may *seem* clear enough, it is not always easy for the courts to decide how to apply it in individual cases, and decisions reached in tribunals or the courts may well be overturned on appeal.

Your rights in civil law
The civil, as distinct from criminal, law covers a wide field. It includes such things as the law of contract, and the law of tort. Tort is an ancient legal term covering a variety of 'civil wrongs' including trespass and libel, and the important field of negligence.

Many cases affecting people at work involve negligence—a carelessly protected machine resulting in the loss of an operative's finger; a carelessly driven company lorry resulting in loss of life, injury or damage to cargo; a badly supervised training area where an inexperienced trainee suffers injury. Negligence is usually a matter for the civil law, where the plaintiff sues the defendant for financial compensation. There is also the offence of **criminal negligence**, but prosecutions are comparatively rare.

Negligence and the duty of care
The essence of civil liability in negligence is that everyone (employer and employee alike) owes a **duty of care** to act reasonably to persons around them.

- The general test applied by the courts is whether a person of reasonable intelligence would have been able to foresee the harm.

Employers and employees who have been trained in a particular profession or skill owe a greater duty to those who rely on them. For example, a doctor might owe a greater duty to an injured pedestrian, than a passer-by with no medical qualifications.

The following case history illustrates one way in which both an employee and his employer might be found by the courts to be negligent.

The case of a negligent teacher
A teacher was employed to teach a class of 25 seven-year olds. The class was well-behaved. It was split into two groups. The teacher set out a number of scissors for one group to take. One child took scissors with a sharp point and suffered an eye injury.

The court decided that the teacher, and his employers, were liable in negligence: sharp scissors should have been avoided unless absolutely necessary, when the danger would have been explained to the children (*Re X, 1988*).

(For the negligence of employers, see Chapter 8, Health and Safety at Work.)

Industrial Tribunals

It is an important feature of modern employment law, that employees are able to take most complaints to an industrial tribunal, rather than to the civil courts. Hearings before an industrial tribunal are generally much quicker, and more informal, without the need for legal representation and heavy legal costs. The tribunals form part of English civil law, and appeals can ultimately be taken to the Court of Appeal, the House of Lords and even to the European Court of Justice (see the chart on page 8). Cases involving important legal points can therefore come before both tribunals and the higher courts.

The following **case history** shows the way in which the courts and tribunals operate in the area of employment, and how the courts deal with difficulties arising from statutes, helping to define or clarify the law in the process.

The case of the part-time teacher
A part-time teacher worked a total of 19½ hours a week. At that time, the qualifying number of hours for a claim for unfair dismissal was 21. She was dismissed by her employers, and claimed compensation for unfair dismissal. Her first claim was in the

industrial tribunal. Her employers argued that she was not entitled to compensation because she did not work the required minimum number of hours. She argued in response that she worked longer hours at home doing preparation, in order to do the job properly.

The tribunal rejected her argument. She then appealed to the Employment Appeal Tribunal on the ground that there was an **implied term** in her contract of employment that she had to work as many hours as necessary to perform her contract properly. This argument was accepted. The employers then appealed to the Court of Appeal on a point of law. The Court upheld the appeal on the basis that the circumstances of each teacher were so different that it was impossible to imply such a vague term. She was not therefore entitled to compensation (*Lake v Essex County Council*, 1979).

A further appeal could have been made to the House of Lords, but it must always be borne in mind that legal proceedings at this level are very expensive and could literally take years.

A word of warning

It is most important for both employers and employees to be aware that legal proceedings in the civil courts, as a general rule, are best avoided:

- Litigation can involve considerable costs and seemingly endless delays.

- Legal aid is not available in tribunals, only in courts.

- Employees and employers are usually both better off trying to settle their differences by negotiation, conciliation and arbitration procedures using legal rules as a guideline.

- Law should be the *last* resort.

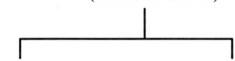

ENGLISH LAW
(Statutes and case law)

CIVIL LAW

Branches of civil law

Law of contract

Tort (civil wrongs such as
negligence, trespass,
defamation)

Property law

Commercial law

Family law

Employment law

Consequences for defendant

Payment of damages

Payment of costs

Obedience to injunctions

CRIMINAL LAW

Branches of criminal law

Offences against the person
(assault, actual or grievous
bodily harm, false imprisonment, rape, murder etc)

Offences against property (theft,
burglary, fraud, deception,
criminal damage etc)

Other offences (eg road traffic
offences, breaches of the
peace, obstructing the police
etc)

Consequences for defendant

Binding over

Probation

Fines

Community service

Custodial sentence

The main branches of English law.

The criminal law at work

The activities of all employers and employees at the workplace are subject to the criminal law. In particular, the following offences may be relevant:

Theft

Technically, this is the dishonest appropriation of property belonging to another. This offence clearly covers the unauthorised physical removal of material from the workplace. It has also been decided that it extends to supermarket workers selling goods to accomplices at reduced prices.

Deception

A range of crimes involving deception can apply to workplace situations. A waiter was found in possession of bottles of wine which he planned to sell to his employer's customers for his own profit: he was convicted of a deception offence.

Cheque and credit card frauds are clear examples of deception offences.

False accounting

The falsification of a document made or required for an accounting purpose is a criminal offence. An employee who falsified accounts to exaggerate the profit made by his department, in order to create a good impression on his employer, was held liable for this offence.

Fiddling expenses might also come under this heading.

Result of criminal acts

A person suspected of a criminal act may well be reported to the police, either by the employer or some other person. An employer would be entitled to dismiss someone convicted of a criminal act involving their employment.

RIGHTS AND DUTIES OF EMPLOYERS AND EMPLOYEES

As an employee, you are normally entitled to a written statement of the terms and conditions of your employment. This may include some kind of summary of the duties you are asked to carry out at work. However, the information may be set out rather sketchily, for example 'short order cook' or 'to be a sales representative for the spare parts division'. Some employers also include a phrase like 'and to carry out any other instructions as the company may give.' Only when the employee has begun work—and sometimes only after quite a long while—do misunderstandings and disputes quite genuinely arise.

Whatever may or may not be included in the contract of employment, the law of the land will ultimately decide what are the duties of employers and employees in particular cases. Such general principles as to act with reasonable care in each other's interests are well-founded in case law, quite apart from any matters which may be set out in a contract of employment, or required eg under health and safety legislation.

Rights of employees

The rights of employees are not set out in any one place. Rather they are protected by a whole range of statutory and common law. The main areas of employees' rights are dealt with chapter by chapter in this book, but this is a general summary of rights which can exist:

- Contractual rights. The right to receive all the benefits from an employer arising from the contract of employment.

- The right to receive fair and reasonable treatment in employment matters.

- The right to certain standards of health and safety at work ('a safe system of work'), underpinned partly by modern legislation such as the Factories Act and Health and Safety at Work Act, and partly by the common law (eg the law relating to negligence).

- The right to equality at work in certain specified fields, for example under the sex and race discrimination laws, and equal pay legislation.

- The right to a written statement of terms and conditions of employment covering such matters as an itemised pay statement, notice arrangements, and grievance/disciplinary procedures.

- The right not to be 'unfairly dismissed' (a right which can be put at risk for example by misconduct or poor job performance).

- The right to belong (or not belong) to a trade union, and the right to remedies if union matters are conducted improperly.

- The right to maternity leave.

- The right to be absent from work for certain public and union duties.

- The right to be paid during periods of absence resulting from sickness or injury.

- The right to seek remedies in the civil courts, or industrial tribunal, or both.

Duties of employees
The general duties of every employee under English law can be summarised as follows:

- To work, unless sick or having some other good excuse.

- To take reasonable care in relation to duties of employment.

- To be reasonably competent.

- To be loyal to the interests of the employer. An employee must act honestly, and must not take secret profit or benefit from confidential information.

Disobedience of employees
An employee is not entitled to disobey the reasonable instructions of the employer in the course of the employment. However, as in so many matters, this is liable to different interpretations. The following case concerns an employee who disobeyed an express order.

The case of the shot-blasting which went wrong
Mr England, a coal miner, assisted the shotsman to set up for shot blasting, even though he was expressly prohibited from doing so. Thinking that Mr England had removed himself safely, the shotsman detonated the explosive. In fact Mr England was very near to the point of the explosion and was injured. Mr England claimed damages on the basis of the employer's liability for the negligence of a co-worker. The employer argued that Mr England had acted entirely outside the scope of his employment, by assisting the shotsman.
    This was rejected by the House of Lords. They decided that the

employer was liable because Mr England had been carrying out the work of a mine worker, even though in a wrong way (*National Coal Board v England, 1954*).

Duties of employer to third parties

An employer may have general duties towards outside firms or individuals, which have a bearing on the conduct of his own employees. It can be the duty of an employer to ensure that his employees behave in a certain manner, as the following case illustrates:

The case of a dishonest employee
A company provided a specialist security protection service at the premises of J Co Ltd. One of the company's employees stole goods from the premises.

The court decided that J Co Ltd was entitled to damages because the employer had been specifically engaged to protect property. He was therefore under a **duty of care** to do so. That duty had been delegated to an employee and the employer was liable, despite the fact that the employee had committed a criminal act. J Co Ltd was entitled to recover the replacement value of the stolen goods plus the costs of investigating the theft (*Johnson & Johnson v CP Security*, 1985).

SCOPE OF EMPLOYMENT

Disputes involving employers and employees often turn on the question of whether the employee's action (or omission) was, or was not, done as part of the job. If it was, the employer may be responsible for any consequences of that act or omission. If it was not, the employee alone may be responsible.

- An employee unsure of the extent of his authority or duties under his contract of employment would be well advised to seek clarification from the employer.

The kind of questions that could arise:
1. Do I need permission to use the van?
2. Surely it is X's job to do that, not mine?
3. Can I make a personal call from the other office?
4. Would you lend me the company car for the weekend if I promise to deliver A's goods on Sunday?

5. Who is responsible if it goes wrong—me, or the head of the department?
6. I thought I was only paid to repair the parking area, not the front steps to the office. It wasn't my fault she broke her leg.
7. Is it alright if I help Mr G out with delivering those dangerous chemicals?
8. I would never have suffered the accident if I hadn't agreed to stay late and help out.

The employer's liability

The liability of the employer could be

- a direct liability or obligation to the employee;
- vicarious liability to a third party for the employee's acts or omissions.

Vicarious liability

Vicarious liability is the name for the legal rule that an employer is normally liable for actions of employees carried out 'during the course of their employment'. This phrase has a highly technical legal meaning and has been interpreted by the courts on many occasions.

The case of the unauthorised telephone calls

A cleaning company had contracted to clean Heasmans offices and equipment. One of its employees made £1,400 worth of unauthorised telephone calls from Heasmans offices, and Heasmans was liable for this amount. The contract between the parties provided that the cleaning company was strictly liable for acts of their employees while on Heasmans premises. Heasmans sued the cleaning company for the money. The county court decided that the cleaning company was vicariously liable for the employee's act. On appeal to the Court of Appeal, however, this decision was reversed. The court decided that the cleaning company could not be vicariously liable for acts committed by an employee wholly outside the scope of his employment, merely because the job provided the employee with an opportunity to commit the act (*Heasmans v Clarity Cleaning*, 1987).

Injuries during the course of employment

The employer may be liable for injuries which occur to an employee during the **course of employment** even if the employee is not engaged in actual work at the time. The following cases illustrate how this might arise.

The case of the slippery floor
Ms D went from her place of work in a factory to clean her teacup at a tap. The area near the tap was slippery due to a spillage of lubricant. She slipped and was injured. She claimed damages from her employer, alleging negligence arising from his failure to keep the area free from slippery substances.

The employer argued that he could not be liable because Ms D had stopped actual work. The court did not accept this. It laid down the rule that an employer's duty to take steps for the safety of employees applies not only during periods of actual work, but also while employees are carrying on activities incidental to their work. Cleaning out a cup was such an incidental activity (*Re D*, 1985).

Injured leaving work
Mr M and Mr S were employed as laggers at a power station. They were instructed to work for a week at another power station. They travelled there in Mr S's car. Shortly before leaving the other power station to go home, they worked for 19 hours and had no sleep at all. During the journey, as a result of Mr S's fatigue, an accident occurred which resulted in Mr M suffering fatal injuries. His widow sued the employer. The House of Lords decided in her favour, and made the following points:

- An employee travelling from home to work is not normally acting in the course of his employment.

- Travelling in the employer's time between workplaces will normally be in the course of employment.

- Where the employee returns home from a place of work other than his base, such a journey is within the course of employment if he was required to make it under his contract of employment.

- If no other transport is available and the employee travels in his own car with the employer's knowledge and approval, that journey may well be in the course of his employment (*Smith v Stages and Darlington Insulation Co Ltd*, 1989).

CONFIDENTIAL INFORMATION

Your work may involve handling information which your employer would naturally want to be treated as confidential. For example, an engineering company might not want its technicians passing information about new products to a competitor; or an employee with a criminal record might not want that information to pass to other employees in the company outside the personnel department.

There is however no single law of privacy or confidentiality to which we can turn. An aggrieved party—whether employee or employer—will have to establish grounds in terms of any relevant statute or case law. For example a technician passing confidential information to outsiders might be in breach of an express or implied term of his contract of employment, giving grounds for dismissal and perhaps even for substantial damages. The employee who suffers harassment as a result of confidential personnel records being released, may be able to claim on grounds of discrimination at work.

An employee's duty of confidentiality
The following case shows how the law relating to confidential matters can be interpreted by the courts.

The case of the polystyrene manufacturer
Mr M worked for a company which had pioneered new methods of manufacturing polystyrene. While on holiday in America he was recruited by an American company. On his return to England he was dismissed. The company sought an **injunction** (court order) to prevent him from divulging information about the new methods.

In the High Court it was found that there was no **restrictive covenant** in the contract of employment to protect the employer. Basic common law principles therefore had to apply. Ex-employees had a continuing **duty of confidentiality**, but this was less than that applying to existing employees. No special information had been given to Mr M. All that he had at his disposal was the general stock of knowledge and experience built up during his working life. The injunction was not granted (*United Sterling Corporation v Felton*, 1974).

Professional advisers and confidentiality
Everyone is entitled to confidentiality in respect of discussions or communications with professional advisers such as a solicitor.

Access to medical reports
Under the **Access to Medical Reports Act 1988** employees have the right of access to any medical report relating to them, supplied by

Reference to Company Doctor

Name:

Address:

Age:

The company wishes to apply to your doctor for a medical report.
You have the following rights under the Access to Medical Reports Act 1988:

(a) not to consent to any application being made to your doctor;
(b) to ask to see any report before disclosure to the company;
(c) to be told when an application for a report is being made;
(d) to stop it being shown to the company or to ask for it to be changed (if you see the report). If the changes are not made and the report is disclosed you have the right to add to it a note of your own;
(e) to ask to see any medical report relating to you supplied by your doctor for employment or insurance purposes in the previous six months. This request should be made direct to your doctor.

There are limited circumstances in which your doctor may refuse to disclose the report to you, e.g. where it would reveal information relating to another individual.

Should you wish to ask to see a report, you should ask your doctor within 21 days of the date of this form. If you do not, then your doctor may disclose the report in any event.

If you do not ask to see the report on this form, you are entitled to change your mind and provided you notify your doctor before the report is supplied, then your doctor cannot supply it until either:

(a) 21 days have passed without you arranging access to the report;
   or
(b) you have consented to the disclosure (if you do arrange access within 21 days)

Please indicate below what you wish to do:

I consent/do not consent to disclosure of my medical history to the company.

I do/do not wish to see any report before it is provided to the company.

I confirm this complies with my rights under the Access to Medical Reports Act 1988.

Signed ....   Date ....

Your Doctor's name: ....

Address: ....

....

their doctor for employment or insurance purposes. Under this Act employees may also refuse their employer access to these records.

Before asking for a medical report from an employee's doctor, the employer must therefore notify the employee, in writing, that the doctor is to be approached. The employee must also be notified of his or her rights. Consent from the employee must be obtained, also in writing, before consulting the doctor.

Employee's rights
- The right to withhold consent for the employer to consult his or her doctor.
- The right to state that he or she wishes to see the report before it is given to the employer.
- The right to request that the report is amended.
- The right to attach a statement to the report.
- The right to refuse the employer access to the report, after the employee has seen it.
- The right to request access to the report, via the doctor, at any time up to six months after it was requested.

Data protection
The **Data Protection Act 1984** imposed a duty on employers, in many cases, to register with the **Registrar of Data Protection**. The rules only apply to identifiable living persons. They do not cover payroll, pension and accounting records.

- Personal data must not be disclosed to persons not entitled to receive it.

Any individual has the right to be informed whether a registered data user is keeping any data relating to him, and to have access to that data.

REFERENCES

It can be very important for someone applying for a job to be able to give one or more references to the prospective employer. The following case equally illustrates

- the right of an employee to a fair reference from his employer;
- the duty of an employer to give an accurate reference.

Mr Lawton was employed by a company for ten years before being made redundant in 1979. He obtained temporary employment and asked the company for a reference. The financial and administrative manager of the company provided a reference which concluded that he would not re-employ Mr Lawton. As a result Mr Lawton was dismissed. He discovered the contents of the reference which he thought were incorrect, and he sued the company for **negligence** (a **tort** or civil wrong).

The High Court decided that the company owed Mr Lawton a **duty of care** to provide an accurate reference. However, on the facts of the case the contents of the reference were honest, accurate and not negligently written (*Lawton v BOC*, 1987).

Questions and answers

1. *Can references be taken up without my consent?*

Yes. English law has no rules about privacy and there is nothing to prevent one person writing a statement about another, provided that it is true.

2. *Do I have a right to know what has been said about me in a reference?*

Yes. If the referee or employer refuses to disclose the contents of a reference, you can get a court order forcing them to do so.

3. *Is my former employer obliged to give a reference if asked, or has he the right to refuse?*

Employees have no legal right to a reference and employers cannot be obliged to give one against their wishes.

BEING A COMPANY DIRECTOR

Where an employer is a limited company, with the advantage of limited liability, the position of the directors is crucially important. A limited company has a legal personality quite separate from that of its members. For example it can own things, and sue and be sued, in its own name. The company is liable to outsiders only to the extent of its own assets, and not the assets of individual members (shareholders).

The complexities of company law are outside the scope of this book, but director-employees should bear in mind the following points:

Number of directors
Every company must have at least one director. A public company (PLC) must have at least two. Their duty is generally to run the company on a day-to-day basis.

Directors' personal guarantees
In some circumstances, directors are asked to provide personal guarantees for company borrowing. This destroys the benefits of limited liability.

Directors acting without authority
A director who commits a company to an act outside its legal powers, and who causes the company loss as a result, may be personally liable for such loss.

Appointment and removal of directors
Directors are appointed and removed by the shareholders at annual or extraordinary general meetings of the company. The appointment and removal of directors is governed by the company's articles of association, which may for example provide for retirement of directors by rotation.

Director acting on behalf of the company
A director may legally bind the company to a third party, for example by entering into a contract, where he has authority to do so. This authority may be expressly written down (for example in minutes of a board meeting, or his contract of employment) or may be implied from the circumstances. A company must take care in choosing its directors and employees because their position may give them implied authority to do acts on their own initiative.

Types of director
It is for the company to decide the particular duties of individual directors; the law is mainly concerned with the legal responsibilities of *all* directors, regardless of what title their company may have bestowed on them. Directors employed as 'managing director', 'sales director', or 'executive director' may have very wide implied authority arising from their title. For example a sales director may be assumed to have

authority to decide prices or discounts. A managing director may be assumed to have greater authority than a sales director, and so on.

Directors' responsibility for company accounts
The Companies Acts set out detailed rules for the proper keeping of books and accounting records. Directors should be aware that failure to observe these rules may result in criminal prosecution. It's probably not enough to say 'I thought the accountant was dealing with it.' Many people who become directors after a career, for example in factory or sales management, are woefully ignorant of their responsibilities and liabilities under modern legislation.

Summary of directors' general legal duties
Directors are often unaware of the scope of their legal duties. A sales director may for example be thinking almost entirely about sales, a personnel director almost entirely about staff. But *all* company directors have the following legal duties:

1. To exercise reasonable skill and care.

2. To give proper time and attention to the company.

3. Not to let his own interest conflict with that of the company.

4. Not to make a secret profit.

5. Not to misapply the company's property.

6. To act bona fide for the benefit of the company as a whole.

Companies Acts rules affecting directors
The **Companies Acts** also contain rules governing directors' duties, including:

- Declarations of interest in contracts with the company.

- Approval of property transactions with the company.

- Restrictions on loans made to directors by the company.

- Disclosure of directors' shareholdings in the company.

Disqualification of company directors

A director may be disqualified by a court order in a number of situations including:

- Conviction of a criminal offence in connection with a company.

- Fraud.

- Being unfit to act as a director.

The following recent cases show how two such situations have been interpreted by the courts.

The director whose company went bust
A director set up two companies which eventually ceased to trade, owing very large sums of money in respect of VAT, income tax, national insurance contributions and general debts. The Official Receiver applied to the court for an order disqualifying him from being a director.

The court decided that his conduct did not warrant disqualification. Such an order should only be made where a director acted cynically to exploit the privilege of limited liability, or in a case of gross incompetence (*Re Stanford Services*, 1987).

The director who traded fraudulently
Mr K was the director of a company selling carbon paper. He fraudulently induced customers to pay for paper which they had not ordered. He was charged with the criminal offence of **fraudulent trading**, under the Companies Acts, and was convicted on the basis that he had intended to defraud the customers. It was not relevant that the customers were not, in the technical sense, creditors of the company.

2
Your Contract of Employment

This Chapter deals with the following:

- the question of whether or not you are an 'employee'
- your right to a written statement of contract
- your rights regarding pay and deductions from pay
- your rights regarding hours of work
- your rights regarding absences from work
- your rights relating to wrongful dismissal

AM I AN 'EMPLOYEE'?

For the vast majority of people at work, the answer is clear enough. They work for an employer, who pays them a wage or salary (less deductions for such things as PAYE and national insurance) and in return carry out their duties of employment. If you are thinking of suing your 'employer' for some reason, or taking him to an Industrial Tribunal, it is clearly important to be sure that you are or were in fact 'employed', since so much of the law and its remedies turn on such phrases as 'was employed by', or 'in the course of employment' and so on.

But surprising as it may seem, there is no one simple test or definition by which it can easily be established whether the relationship of employer and employee exists in any particular case. Consider the following:

A and B are friends. A helps B each week by delivering B's commercial goods to Norwich, because A has a girlfriend in Norwich and it's on his way. B usually gives A some money for his trouble. Unfortunately, on one trip A runs down a pedestrian who, seeing B's name on the side of the van sues B, claiming that B is vicariously liable for the injury caused in the course of his employment by A.

But is A employed by B, or not? The search for such a test seems to be a false errand. The possible permutations of conditions under which one person works for another are probably too many and varied to be wrapped up in a brief legal expression. The courts in dealing with the awkward facts of cases before them, after years of struggle to find an apt definition, have produced a so-called 'multiple' test. The **legal questions to ask** are:

- Have the parties described themselves as employer and employee in any contract?

- Must the person working provide his own skill?

- Does the employer have a sufficient degree of control in respect of manner, time and place of work?

- Who provides the tools, equipment and premises?

- Who takes the financial risk?

- Who takes the chance of profit?

- Who pays PAYE and National Insurance?

Here is an example of a case deciding whether or not someone was 'employed'.

The case of the sacked TV reporter
A television reporter had a number of contracts with a television company to provide her services as a reporter. The contracts were of fixed terms linked to the particular programmes she was working on. When she started to work for the company, her accountant wrote confirming that, for income tax purposes, she was to be treated as self-employed. No tax was ever deducted from her salary. Under the terms of her contract, copyright in her work was vested in the television company, she agreed to observe company house rules and to work as required and directed by the programme producer.

A new producer was appointed. He did not like the reporter's voice and he decided not to renew her contract. She claimed that this amounted to unfair dismissal. The television company argued that since she was not an employee, there could be no unfair dismissal.

The court decided that she *was* an employee, despite the

STATEMENT OF MAIN TERMS AND CONDITIONS OF EMPLOYMENT

as required by the Employment Protection (Consolidation) Act 1978

Name of business	ACME SECRETARIAL SERVICES
Name of employee	MR. X
Branch or Department	SALES OFFICE
Date employment began (*if there has been continuous employment with a previous firm, e.g. on an amalgamation, the date when the previous employment began*).	1/1/91
Job title	OFFICE ADMINISTRATOR
Brief job description	GENERAL CLERICAL DUTIES
Remuneration (*how calculated and whether monthly or weekly, etc.*)	£800 PER MONTH
Normal working hours	40 HOURS PER WEEK
Holidays and holiday pay	SEE COMPANY SCHEME
Provision for sickness or injury	SEE COMPANY SCHEME
Details of the firm's pension scheme (other than the statutory scheme) and whether a certificate of contracting out is in force	Not applicable No certificate as to contracting out is in force
Notice of termination required from (a) the firm (b) the employee	(a) During first year, 1 week's notice, 1 further week's notice for each additional year up to 12 years' maximum (b) 1 week's notice during first year. Thereafter, 2 weeks' notice
Details of disciplinary procedure*	A copy has been received by the employee
Details of grievance procedure*	Ditto

*These may be done by incorporation of other documents and, if so, reference should be made here to the other documents.

I agree that the above represent the agreed terms and conditions of employment and acknowledge receipt of the documents referred to above.

Signed .... Mr. X ....

arrangements regarding payment and taxation of her earnings. On the facts of the case, her contract had all the elements and appearance of a contract of employment (*Thames Television v Wallis*, 1979).

WRITTEN STATEMENT OF MAIN TERMS AND CONDITIONS

A summary required by law

Within 13 weeks of the start of employment, an employer must provide the employee with written particulars of the terms of employment. This must contain the following details

- Name of employer and employee.
- Date of commencement of employment.
- Job title.
- Hours worked.
- Terms of holidays and holiday pay.
- Details of notice of termination.
- Disciplinary and grievance procedures.
- Sickness or injury provisions.
- Pension arrangements.
- If the contract is for a fixed term, the date of expiry.

Is the written statement my contract of employment?
No. The written statement is one specific document required by the employment legislation. It may form part, but not necessarily the whole, of the contract. The relationship between every employer and employee is a contract, and therefore subject to the general law relating to contract, for example:

- The word 'contract' means the relationship into which the parties have entered with the intention that it should be legally binding on each of them.

- A contract arises when one party makes an offer, and the other party signifies its acceptance.

- With certain exceptions a contract does not have to be in writing. It is what the parties believed they agreed that matters. The agreement may cover a range of points, perhaps discussed at several different times, and partly evidenced in writing and partly not. If one party sues another for breach of contract the

---

ACME SECRETARIAL SERVICES

Written statement under the Employment Protection (Consolidation) Act 1978
1. You are employed as an office administrator.
2. Pay will be £800 per month.
3. Your normal working hours will be 40 per week.
4. Your holiday and sickness arrangements will be as set out in the company's scheme.
5. Disciplinary rules are set out in a separate document.

Written Statement of Terms and Conditions of Employment
(Short form)

The notice you have to give to terminate your employment is one calendar month unless more is required in the particular case by an attached addendum.

The notice you are entitled to receive to terminate your employment is one calendar month increasing after four years of employment by one week for each succeeding full year of employment up to a maximum of twelve weeks' notice except where otherwise provided for.

The Company may require you to take paid leave of absence during all or any part of a period of notice.

Example of Notice requirements

court will have to consider the whole matter to try and establish exactly what was agreed. Obviously, the more the terms and conditions are spelled out in writing, the less opportunity there should be for misunderstanding or dispute (in theory at least).

However, it is certainly helpful both to employer and employee to have the written statement as required by law, since it must include so many matters of obvious importance to each.

Unacceptable terms and conditions
1. A contract of employment cannot require an employee to break the law, or put himself at undue risk.

2. A contract of employment cannot seek to 'oust the jurisdiction of the courts', thereby denying the employee any legal remedy to which he is entitled under the law of the land.

3. Under the *Unfair Contract Terms Act 1977*, an employer cannot restrict his liability for death or personal injury to an employee, resulting from the employer's negligence.

Job title
The written statement of terms of employment must specify the title of the job which the employee is employed to do. But what if the job specification is unclear, or altered later?

A woman was taken on as a 'copy typist/general duties clerk'. At first her duties were mainly clerical and typing, but later her employer asked her to operate the duplicator. After agreeing to do this, the woman found that the vapour given off from the machine made her feel ill. There were no other jobs in the woman's department but she was invited to apply for one in the Accounts department. She declined and was dismissed. She claimed unfair dismissal, arguing that her employer was in breach of contract in insisting that she operate the duplicator.

The **Employment Appeal Tribunal** held that her claim must fail. In the context of the case, with a small clerical staff in a small office, the ambit of general duties was enough to include the operation of a duplicator (*Glitz v Watford Electric Co*, 1979).

Date:

Name: Payroll No.:

National Insurance No:

Tax code:

Tax week/month:

Gross pay

Basic pay for period:	£	
Overtime:	£	
Commission/bonus:	£	
SSP/SMP:	£	
Other payments:	£	
TOTAL GROSS PAY:	£	
Pension contribution:	£	
Additional Voluntary Contribution:	£	

TOTAL TAXABLE PAY	£	

Deductions

Tax:	£	
National Insurance:	£	
Other deductions:	£	
TOTAL DEDUCTIONS:	£	

NET PAY FOR PERIOD:	£	

An example of an itemised pay statement.

PAY AND DEDUCTIONS

Itemised pay statement and deductions
Employees have a statutory right to an **itemised pay statement containing the following:**

- Gross and net amounts of wages
- Amounts of deductions

What constitutes 'pay'?
It can be rather important sometimes to know which amounts are for 'pay' and which amounts may be for something else. The following case helps to show what is considered to be an employee's pay and what is not.

Why a tribunal refused an award
Ms D was summarily dismissed from employment as a recruitment consultant. She was a given a cheque in lieu of notice. The cheque was later stopped. She was also owed £55.50 in respect of unpaid commission and holiday pay. She claimed for all this money to the industrial tribunal.

It was held that the stopped cheque did not amount to 'wages' and the industrial tribunal could not deal with the matter. Ms D would have to apply to the county court instead for damages for wrongful dismissal. But she could recover the £55.50 by applying to the tribunal (*Delaney v Staples*, 1991).

Amount of pay
The amount of your pay may be determined by:

- what you agreed with your employer in the contract of employment;
- a union agreement;
- a Wages Council.

Wages Councils were formed to raise the minimum wages payable in a number of industries. **Wages inspectors** ensure that the conditions set by the Wages Council are honoured. Where it is felt that collective bargaining will be effective in setting the rates of pay, either unions or employers can apply to have the Wages Council for that industry abolished.

Deductions from pay

The **Wages Act 1986** provides that deductions may not be made from wages without statutory power or the agreement of the employee. Where an unauthorised deduction has been made, an employee may apply to an industrial tribunal for repayment.

Employers are required by law to deduct the following:

- Tax, for example under the operation of a PAYE scheme.
- Employee's National Insurance contributions.
- Attachment of earnings.

Attachment of earnings

The Attachment of Earnings Act 1971 applies only in England and Wales. It comes into effect when a person has **defaulted on a court order** to pay a debt, fine, or maintenance, by means of regular payments. The courts may make an attachment order for the person's employer to make the deductions and forward them to the court.

Can my pay be cut?

Once the amount of your pay has been agreed it cannot be reduced without your agreement (except for authorised deductions as above). If it is reduced, for example because your employer says he has to 'cut overheads', you may have a good claim for constructive dismissal.

Can I insist on being paid in cash?

In 1986 Parliament passed the Wages Act. This repealed the Truck Acts and as a result manual workers no longer have the statutory right to be paid in coin of the realm (unless they were paid in this way before the new law).

The case of the dinner ladies' pay cut

Six dinner ladies each received a letter from the council which employed them, informing them that because of government controls on local authority spending, their wages would have to be cut. The council said that this was the only way to ensure their continued employment. The ladies rejected the reduction in pay and claimed damages.

The court decided that the letter had been a fundamental breach of contract, and the ladies were entitled to damages (*Burdett-Coutts v Hertfordshire County Council*, 1984).

The following case histories give examples of the kind of deduction which may be made from an employee's wages.

Shortages in a petrol station

Mr Bristow worked as a petrol station cashier. His contract of employment provided that he would make good his share of cash and stock losses occurring during his shift, whether or not such losses were caused by his actions, by deductions from his wages. During the five weeks which he worked for the company, substantial sums were deducted from his wages. He argued that such deductions were 'fines' within the meaning of the Truck Act 1896. This argument was rejected in the magistrates' court. Mr Bristow then appealed to the Divisional Court which rejected the appeal. He then made a further appeal to the House of Lords.

It was held that the word 'fine' in the Act of 1896 meant a financial loss to an employee, agreed upon by employer and employee in cases where part of the contract of employment had not been fulfilled. The deductions did not have to be 'punitive', and in the present case they amounted to a fine (*Bristow v City Petroleum*, 1987).

Refusal to do certain work on a Saturday

Mr Miles was a superintendent registrar of births, deaths and marriages. He normally worked on Saturday mornings. On the instructions of his trade union, he refused to carry out marriages on a Saturday morning. His employer stated that if he did not work as normal he would not be paid. Mr Miles carried out other work on Saturday mornings. His employer withheld a proportion of his pay, effectively not paying him for Saturday mornings.

His action for damages for lost wages was dismissed. He successfully appealed to the Court of Appeal. The employer appealed to the House of Lords. It was held that if Mr Miles declined to do the work for which he was employed, his employer need not pay him (*Miles v Wakefield Metropolitan District Council*, 1987).

HOURS OF WORK

There are no general regulations about hours of work, but certain **statutory regulations** cover particular matters, eg mining. Hours of work can also be regulated by trade union agreements or by the terms of employment agreed individually.

Office workers

There are no rules regarding office workers' hours.

Shop workers
There are rules about early closing, and about the time which may be worked without a break.

Factory workers
Strict rules govern the hours which may be worked by employees under 18, as outlined in the Factories Act 1961. But there are, in general, no statutory limitations regarding the working hours of adults.

Drivers
Drivers of goods vehicles of more than 3.5 tonnes gvw must observe strict regulations as to their hours of driving. Records must be kept. For further details see EC regulations 3820/85, 3821/85 and The Driver's Hours (Goods Vehicles) (Keeping of Records) Regulations 1987.

Young people and children
Young people are defined by law as being between 16 and 18 years old. In several work situations, other than those mentioned above, there are regulations limiting their hours of work.

Youngsters under the school leaving age are defined as 'children'. No child under 13 may be employed; the periods and times which children over the age of 13 are allowed to work are regulated. The regulations do not apply to 'work experience' if it is part of the child's approved education.

Overtime
Generally speaking, exactly the same principles apply to work done in overtime as in normal time.

Do I have a right to work overtime?
An employee has no general right to work overtime unless such a right is specifically embodied in the contract of employment. It is normally a matter of overtime being offered on a regular or occasional basis by the employer, and of the employee agreeing to work it on the terms offered.

Am I obliged to work overtime if asked?
Unless there is some provision in the contract of employment, an employee is not bound to work for more hours than the number of

hours agreed in the contract of employment. Even so, disputes can arise even where overtime is covered in a contract of employment, as the following case shows:

The case of the overworked doctor
Dr Johnstone was employed as a senior house officer. His contract of employment provided for 40 hours a week overtime in addition to his normal hours. He applied to the High Court for a declaration that he could not lawfully be made to work more than 72 hours a week, because his health might be damaged. The application was refused, and he appealed to the Court of Appeal.

The appeal succeeded. The employer could not require an employee to do so much overtime that his health might be damaged *(Johnstone v Bloomsbury Health Authority*, 1990).

ABSENCE FROM WORK

You may be, or wish to be, absent from work for a number of reasons, for example:

- sickness or injury
- union activities
- public duties
- military duties
- compassionate grounds
- domestic obligations

You have the statutory right to paid or unpaid absence for some, but not all, of these reasons. (Maternity leave is explained on page 89.)

Absence through sickness or injury
If you are obliged to be absent from work as a result of sickness or injury, you may be entitled to receive Statutory Sick Pay (SSP) from your employer. Your entitlement is based on your gross earnings for up to 28 weeks of any period of incapacity for work. After that you may have to claim state benefits.

These are minimum entitlements guaranteed by law. Some employers offer more generous arrangements under a **company sick pay scheme**, which may form part of your contract of employment.

Exclusions for SSP
You do not have a statutory right to SSP if:

- you are ill outside the EEC countries
- you are ill during an industrial dispute with your employer
- you are above pensionable age
- you are earning less than the national insurance lower earnings limit

Qualifying for SSP

Employees are entitled to SSP after a three day 'waiting period' without payment. An employee has to be off work for at least four **qualifying days** to receive any payment. Qualifying days are those on which an employee would normally work.

If an employee is off work due to sickness, following a period of incapacity within the previous eight weeks, the two periods are linked and treated as one SSP period. Three waiting days are not then needed for the subsequent absence. However, this subsequent absence must also be of at least four days for payment to be made.

After seven days' absence, including days not usually worked, a medical certificate from a doctor is required. Otherwise self-certification is sufficient.

SSP and tax

SSP is treated as earnings for the purposes of national insurance and PAYE.

Malingering

An employee abusing the sickness scheme may render himself liable to disciplinary action by the employer, who may in certain circumstances withhold SSP.

Absence for public duties

You have a right to be absent from work in order to discharge public duties if you are:

- a Justice of the Peace
- a member of a local authority
- a member of a statutory tribunal
- a member of a regional or district Health Authority (Health Board in Scotland)
- called for jury service
- a school or college governor

However, you are not entitled to be paid by your employer during such absences. (Some employers may choose not to exercise their right to withhold pay for such absences.) Public bodies generally pay some expenses to individuals who serve them. Jurors for example may claim allowances for subsistence, travel and financial loss from the courts.

The right to paid time off
You have the right to be paid by your employer for reasonable amounts of time off for

- union representation and training
- health and safety representation and training
- looking for a new job, or arranging training, if you are under notice of redundancy
- for ante-natal care if pregnant

No right to time off
Unless agreed in your contract of employment, or allowed by your employer, you have no automatic right to time off for

- marriages, christenings, bereavements or funerals
- moving house
- paternity
- Territorial Army or similar commitments

unless you can arrange to take it as holiday entitlement.

WRONGFUL DISMISSAL

Wrongful dismissal occurs where an employee is dismissed with less notice than he is entitled to receive under his contract of employment, or is dismissed before the expiry of a fixed term contract. In other words it involves **breach of contract** and therefore comes under the civil law.

Damages for wrongful dismissal should normally be claimed in the county court.

- This is an independent and separate claim from any claim to the Industrial Tribunal for **unfair dismissal**.

The case of a dismissed social worker

Mrs Dietman was a senior social worker. Following the death of Jasmine Beckford she was criticised by a panel of inquiry and was instantly dismissed without notice or pay in lieu. She was given no opportunity to state her case.

The Council's disciplinary procedure provided that employees were entitled to a hearing. It was further provided that certain types of gross misconduct could lead to instant dismissal. 'Gross misconduct' was defined as 'misconduct of such a nature that the authority is justified in no longer tolerating the continued presence at the place of work of the employee'.

Mrs Dietman lodged an appeal under the Council's disciplinary procedure, claiming that her dismissal had been wrongful. This was turned down. Later, she accepted a job with Wolverhampton Borough Council. She then brought an action in the county court, claiming damages for wrongful dismissal, and an injunction to stop the Council from dismissing her.

In the county court, it was held that she had been wrongfully dismissed. However, her acceptance of other employment amounted to acceptance of the wrongful dismissal. She was not entitled to an injunction, but she could recover damages. The Council appealed to the Court of Appeal. That Court decided that the dismissal had been wrongful. Her 'gross negligence' had not amounted to 'gross misconduct', and in any event there should have been a formal disciplinary meeting (*Dietman v London Borough of Brent*, 1988).

Bad language costs gardener his job

Mr Wilson was the head gardener on Mr Racher's estate. He was employed on terms which guaranteed him not less than six months' employment. Six weeks after starting work the two men had a row during which Mr Wilson made the following remarks:

'Get stuffed'; 'Go and sh– yourself'; 'Do you expect me to get f— wet?'

He was dismissed.

He claimed damages for wrongful dismissal, and was awarded £421.15 in the county court. Mr Racher appealed to the Court of Appeal, arguing that Mr Wilson's language fully justified instant dismissal.

The appeal would be dismissed. Mr Wilson's language, though strong, was an isolated outburst drawn from him by provocation. It did not justify dismissal (*Wilson v Racher, 1974*).

Misconduct as grounds for instant dismissal

The Court of Appeal made the following general statement in the above case: 'There is no rule of thumb to determine what misconduct on the part of a servant justifies summary termination of his contract. For the purpose of the present case the test is whether the plaintiff's conduct was insulting and insubordinate to such a degree as to be incompatible with the continuance of the relationship of master and servant.'

3
Disciplinary Procedures

This chapter deals with the following subjects:

- Codes of Practice
- Disciplinary Rules
- Gross misconduct
- Grievance procedures

THE ACAS CODE OF PRACTICE

The **Advisory, Conciliation and Arbitration Service (ACAS)** Code of Practice on Disciplinary Practice and Procedures gives a framework for disciplinary and grievance procedures. It has been described as having a similar status to the Highway Code—it is not part of the law, but breach of its rules may result in an application to a Tribunal.

This Specimen Disciplinary Procedure follows the guidelines of the ACAS Code of Practice. It aims to set out very clear rules, thus restricting the number of possible disputes.

Disciplinary Procedure
(A) Disciplinary Procedure Involving Gross Misconduct
1. Where gross misconduct is alleged, the employee will immediately be suspended on full pay pending an investigation. That investigation will, as far as is practicable, be carried out within two working days. The employee's union representative and the personnel manager will be notified immediately. After investigation, the employee will be interviewed with his union representative or a fellow employee of his choice present, if he requires it. He will be given an opportunity of stating his case.

2. After the matter has been considered by management, the employee will be notified of the result. This will involve one of the following:

(a) written warning that further conduct of a similar nature will result in dismissal;

or (b) notice of termination of employment;

or (c) summary dismissal;

or (d) suspension without pay;

or (e) no further action will be taken and all record of the matter will be cancelled.

(B) Disciplinary Procedure in Cases Not Involving Gross Misconduct

1. The employer's manager will investigate the facts fully and interview the employee. The employee's union representative will be notified. The employee will, when appropriate, be reprimanded and given a warning.

   A warning will have the effect that, if no improvement occurs within one month, Stage 2 of this procedure may then take place. If, as is hoped, improvement does occur within that period, then the warning is cancelled and no record will be kept.

2. If no improvement occurs within one month, a formal oral warning will be given that further conduct of a similar nature, or continued failure to meet the standard required, will result in a final warning. The employee will be allowed a specific period within which to improve.

   A record will be kept by the manager concerned. A copy will also be kept by the personnel manager on the employee's personal file. The employee's trade union representative will also have been informed.

3. If there is still no improvement within the time specified, a formal final warning will be given. This will indicate that further conduct of a similar nature or, where appropriate, failure to meet the required standard within a specified period, will result in termination of the employment. That formal final warning will be confirmed in writing and a copy kept by the personnel manager and the employee's union representative.

   If there has been a continuous improvement in the employee's conduct, this disciplinary step will, in the ordinary course of events, be cancelled after a period of between six and nine months. However, there may be circumstances in which a subsequent repetition of the misconduct will result in this stage being carried out immediately without a previous oral warning.

4. If unfortunately the employee continues to fail to meet the requirement set out in the previous warnings he will be given written notice terminating his employment. Again it is open to the employee to have his trade union representative or a fellow employee present at any meeting or interview arranged before dismissal.

Appeals
The employee may appeal against disciplinary action at any stage of this procedure. This appeal is to the next higher level of management not involved in any previous step. It must be made in writing within three working days. If no appeal is made in this way, it will be assumed that the disciplinary decision has been accepted by the employee.

Other actions
Action may also be brought against employers for breach of rules, for example the **Health and Safety at Work Act**.

CODE OF PRACTICE 1: BASIC PRINCIPLES

Contents of disciplinary procedures

- Persons affected.

- Provision for speedy resolution of disciplinary matters.

- List of actions which may be taken.

- Levels of management with authority to take steps.

- Rule that employees should be able to state their case before disciplinary decisions are reached.

- Statement of right of employee to be accompanied at disciplinary hearing.

- Provision that no instant dismissal except for gross misconduct.

- Rule that no disciplinary action to be taken without full investigation.

- Provision for explanation of penalties to employee.

- Right of appeal.

These procedures should only be brought into effect after consultation with trade unions.

DISCIPLINARY RULES

If you work for a large organisation there will almost certainly be a set of staff rules perhaps in the form of a Staff Rulebook or notices prominently displayed on the premises. As we have already seen, you are entitled by law to receive details of disciplinary and grievance procedures within 13 weeks of starting work, as part of your written statement of terms and conditions of employment.

The existence of such rules, if reasonable and kept to a minimum, should normally be a help to employees as much as employers, since they help to clarify subjects which can easily become the cause of misunderstandings and grievances. The rules will of course depend on the nature of the organisation and what it does, but these are the kinds of topics commonly covered:

Health and safety
What is the company's policy on health and safety matters? This is covered in detail in Chapter 8.

Smoking
Is smoking permitted on the premises? Is it permitted generally, or only in certain places (eg canteen) and at certain times? Are some areas designated non-smoking areas?

Alcohol
What is the employer's policy on the consumption of alcohol on the premises? Is it permitted, or banned completely? What about mildly alcoholic drinks like shandies?

Food and drink
Is the consumption of food and drink limited to certain times and places?

Absences
For a discussion of this, see pages 39-41.

Time-keeping
How punctual must you be arriving at work? What is likely to happen if you habitually arrive five minutes late and leave five minutes early? Is there a policy on flexihours? How does it operate? How is time-keeping dealt with in the disciplinary procedures?

Work standards
Are there any written details as to the standard or amount of work required from you? Your written statement of terms and conditions of employment may only refer to this briefly. Are several employees working to the same standard in the same job, or are you expected to work to an individual standard?

Use of company vehicle
If you have access to a company car or commercial vehicle, what limitations are there on its use? Can you use it for domestic purposes? What is the insurance cover? What are the arrangements for purchasing fuel? Even if you have a 'company car', can the management make you share it with someone else if it chooses?

Private telephone calls
What use if any is permitted of company phones for personal calls? With the advent of modern technology, many firms now obtain computer printouts from British Telecom showing all calls made, their duration, time, and cost incurred, linked to extension numbers.

Car parking
Are certain parking areas reserved?

Misconduct and gross misconduct
For a discussion of these see pages 49-52.

Your right to understand any disciplinary rules
An employee is entitled to a clear knowledge of disciplinary rules.

- It is not enough for an employer to make an agreement with a trade union and leave it to the union to inform the employee.

The following case illustrates the point.

The case of the Christmas party hangover
During a Christmas party given by the Company, Mr X had a little

too much to drink. He and several other employees failed to turn up for work on the following day. Before the next Christmas party, the Company negotiated a special rule with the trade union, that failure to report for work on the day after the party would result in summary dismissal. Mr X over-indulged again and failed to report for work the next day. He was dismissed, and made a claim for unfair dismissal. The company's case was that all of the employees had been verbally warned that failure to report for work would result in instant dismissal, and that they all knew the rule very well. Mr X said that his impression was that the penalty was only the loss of a day's pay.

The tribunal decided that before enforcing any special disciplinary rule, an employer must have clear evidence that employees had been informed of the rule, and of the penalty for infringing it, in writing. It was not enough simply to make the agreement with a trade union and leave it to the union to inform the employees (*Brooks & Son v Skinner*, 1984).

GROSS MISCONDUCT

Definition
Gross misconduct means serious misconduct meriting instant dismissal. Such misconduct could take many forms, for example:

- violence or fighting at work
- foul language and intimidating or antisocial behaviour
- dishonesty
- indecent behaviour
- obviously criminal acts

The question of what constitutes gross misconduct in particular cases can be a matter of dispute, which may then come before an industrial tribunal. The employee may not have realised that the action complained of would be regarded by his employer as gross misconduct.

An employer may define what it means by gross misconduct in its disciplinary rules. It is probably helpful both to employer and employee alike to have a clear statement of some kind. The following is an example.

Disciplinary Rules: Gross Misconduct
'Where an act of misconduct is regarded by management as so

fundamental to the operation of the Company or its industrial relations that it would be inappropriate to give a warning prior to consideration of dismissal it will be treated as gross misconduct above.

'Examples which, when these issues affect the Company, will normally be regarded as gross misconduct are as follows:

- Unauthorised disclosure of Company information.
- Behaviour prejudicial to the good name of the Company.
- Gross negligence or insubordination.
- Theft or fraud.
- Violent behaviour.
- Wilful breach of safety regulations, endangering the safety of other persons or equipment.
- Wilful damage to Company property.
- Offensive behaviour or language.
- Drunkenness.
- Dishonesty.
- Drug abuse.
- Betting or gambling on Company property.

'These are examples only and this is not an exhaustive list.'

Dishonesty as gross misconduct
The following recent case involved this very point.

Unauthorised use of confidential information
Mr J was a sheet metal worker and a shop steward. He had his own password which allowed him entry to his employers' computer, thus gaining access to engineering information. He was accused by the employers of using another employee's password to obtain access to information which would be of use to his trade union activities and against the interests of the company. He was summarily dismissed and complained of unfair dismissal to an industrial tribunal.

The tribunal decided that the employers had acted reasonably. On appeal to the **Employment Appeal Tribunal** however this decision was reversed. The EAT stated that if an employee deliberately used an unauthorised password in order to gain computerised information, that was gross misconduct which would attract summary dismissal. It was important that management should make it abundantly clear that interfering with computers would carry severe penalties (*Re J*, 1990).

Dishonestly clocking unworked hours
The offence of falsely clocking unworked hours is an example of dishonesty which is considered by industrial tribunals to be serious enough to merit instant dismissal.

Mr Stewart, a one-man bus driver, was seen to hand in his cash and ticket dispenser at 7 am when his shift was supposed to end at 9.45. He claimed to have worked a full shift. The company's disciplinary procedure required an employee to be warned of the consequences of such an offence as soon as it came to light. Mr Stewart was in fact allowed to commit the offence twice. He was then dismissed.

The industrial tribunal held that the dismissal had been fair. The offence of falsely clocking unworked hours was so serious that instant dismissal could be justified (*Stewart v Western SMT Co Ltd*, 1978).

Violence as gross misconduct
Fighting at work is always a serious matter and will often constitute gross misconduct, depending on the circumstances of the case.

The refusal that offended
Mr McLoughlin, a shop steward, asked another employee, Mr D, to do some extra work to fill in for an absentee. Mr D refused. An argument developed into a fight, and Mr D was hospitalised. After an investigation Mr McLoughlin was dismissed. His work record had been good until the events leading to the dismissal. The tribunal found that the fight had not been gross misconduct and had not justified summary dismissal. The employer appealed to the Employment Appeal Tribunal which found that the dismissal had been fair. The question was, had the employer acted reasonably? Fighting was always a serious matter, especially when machinery was nearby, and an employer was usually well justified in dismissing for fighting (*Parsons & Co Ltd v McLoughlin*, 1978).

Indecency as gross misconduct
Indecent behaviour at work may have consequences for the employer and other staff under the Sex Discrimination Act.

An employee may be liable to lose his job after being found guilty of gross indecency at work.

Indecency away from work
The same may apply even if the offence takes place outside work, as was illustrated by a case in Nottinghamshire involving a school

teacher. Mr Bowly, a schoolteacher for thirty years, pleaded guilty to a charge of gross indecency in a public lavatory. After an inquiry he was dismissed from his post. The industrial tribunal found that he was a man of homosexual tendencies which he tried to resist. There was no evidence of any such activity with any pupils.

The industrial tribunal found that the dismissal had been unfair. The employer appealed to the Employment Appeal Tribunal. The appeal was upheld. The dismissal had *not* been unfair. It was up to the employer to decide how he would react to sexual behaviour of this kind. In the present case, the employer had investigated the matter carefully and thoroughly (*Nottinghamshire County Council v Bowly*, 1978).

Misconduct other than gross

We have seen that gross misconduct may entitle the employer to dismiss the employee instantly. But of course not all misconduct is 'gross' by any means. In the average factory, shop or office, such things as lateness or unexplained absences may be a more common cause of concern.

GRIEVANCE PROCEDURES

Every employee is entitled to have the grievance procedure explained to them in their written statement of terms and conditions of employment, or set out in a written or printed document of some kind.

Grievance procedure for gross misconduct

An employer may set out a detailed grievance procedure covering gross misconduct. The following is an example:

1. In cases which management believes to be gross misconduct the employee will be suspended from work pending a hearing.

2. Where, following that hearing, management is satisfied that dismissal is appropriate it will be immediate and without notice. It may be without notice pay and the period of suspension will not be paid.

3. Where management decides that dismissal is not appropriate, but that disciplinary action is justified, it may substitute a warning and

the period of suspension may be paid or not as management deems appropriate. In addition, a further period of suspension may be imposed which shall not exceed five working days and which shall be unpaid.

4. Where management decides that disciplinary action was inappropriate the period of suspension will be paid and the action expunged from the employee's records.

Grievance procedure for other matters

Here is a typical grievance procedure for employees wishing to make complaints:

Specimen grievance procedure for complaints
1. Any employee wishing to complain by way of grievance must first raise the matter with his or her immediate superior.
2. If it cannot be resolved it will be referred to Ms X for her to resolve.
3. If it cannot be dealt with at that level, it will be referred to Ms Y for a final decision.
4. The company will endeavour to establish all facts relating to the complaint as soon as is practicable.

Most complaints are best resolved personally, but every employee has the right to representation by a fellow employee or a trade union official at all stages of this procedure.

The three-stage disciplinary process

For misconduct other than gross, the following three stage disciplinary process should normally apply:

- spoken warning
- written warning
- final written warning

The following sequence sets out how the employer should proceed in such a matter.

Specimen warning letter

Dear Mr X
In view of your continued lateness and unexplained absences from

work, despite several oral warnings, I must now formally warn you that unless matters improve, your conduct will be treated as a disciplinary matter with all possible consequences this may entail.

Yours faithfully

Specimen final warning letter

Dear Mr X

One month ago you were sent a formal warning letter in relation to your consistent lateness and unexplained absences from work. In view of the fact that your timekeeping and attendance record has not improved, and that you have been late for work twelve times during the past month, I must now inform you that any repetition of this behaviour will be treated as a breach of your contract of employment, and you will be dismissed.

Yours faithfully

Specimen dismissal letter

Dear Mr X

Despite two formal letters of warning in relation to your lateness and unexplained absences from work, your behaviour has not improved. You have been late for work on a further ten occasions. In view of this I have no alternative but to dismiss you from the post of Office Administrator, with effect from four weeks from the date of this letter, in accordance with your contract of employment.

Yours faithfully

4
Unfair Dismissal

This chapter covers the following points:

- your statutory right not to be unfairly dismissed
- the conditions for claiming unfair dismissal
- what 'continuity of employment' means
- dismissal for misconduct
- dismissal for poor job performance
- the amount of awards for unfair dismissal

STATUTORY RIGHT NOT TO BE UNFAIRLY DISMISSED

The 1971 law regarding unfair dismissal

The first legal protection against **unfair dismissal** was created in 1971. Before then, a dismissed employee's only remedy was to go to court to show breach of his employment contract by the employer; he would claim damages (financial compensation) or ask the court to issue an order for reinstatement at work.

The right to sue for breach of contract still exists in the civil courts, but making a claim to a tribunal for unfair dismissal is far more popular for the following reasons:

- it is very much quicker—a court case could take years;

- it is very much cheaper—a court case could cost thousands of pounds;

- it is much less formal—the hearing is before a tribunal rather than a court.

Where dismissal is admitted by the employer, then the employer must show that the reason for the dismissal fell within one of these categories:

1. Misconduct by the employee.
2. Poor capability or qualifications of the employee.
3. Redundancy.
4. Unlawfulness, for example someone employed as an HGV driver lost his licence.
5. Some other substantial reason.

The Tribunal will then consider whether the dismissal was unfair, depending on

> 'Whether in the circumstances (including the size and resources of the undertaking) the employer acted reasonably or unreasonably in treating it as a sufficient reason for dismissing the employee; and that question shall be determined in accordance with equity and with the substantial merits of the case'. (Section 57 of the **Employment Protection (Consolidation) Act 1978**, as amended.)

Wide discretion for tribunals

This section gives a very wide discretion to tribunals hearing cases of alleged wrongful dismissal. What were the 'circumstances'? Did the employer act reasonably, or not? Was the employee treated fairly or unfairly in the matter? What are the 'substantial merits' of the case? While there may be common factors in many cases, the actual details are never quite the same, and only after looking at all the facts in an individual case can a tribunal reach a decision. Here are two fairly recent cases alleging wrongful dismissal, which came before tribunals.

A heated exchange

Mr Tanner had been lent £275 by his employer to buy himself a car. This was to save Mr Tanner having to use the company van for non-business purposes. He was caught using the company van in the evening. His boss said: ' What's my f— van doing outside? You're a tight bastard. I've just lent you £275 to buy a car and you're too tight to put juice in it. That's it, you're finished with me'. Mr Tanner left and claimed unfair dismissal.

The Industrial Tribunal decided that, in the circumstances, the boss's outburst had been an 'angry reprimand' rather than a 'dismissal'. Mr Tanner had not been dismissed and could not claim compensation for unfair dismissal. This decision was confirmed by the Employment Appeal Tribunal (*Tanner v Kean*, 1978).

The EAT made the following general comment: 'The test which has to be applied is as follows: Were the words spoken those of dismissal, that is to say were they intended to bring the contract of employment to an end? What was the employer's intention? In answering that a relevant, and perhaps the most important question, is how would a reasonable employee, in all the circumstances, have understood what the employer intended by what he said and did?'

Dismissal and striking employees
Thirty-five employees went on strike in protest against their employer's dismissal of two union activists. Two of the strikers were allowed to return to work. Ms Stock, one of the remaining strikers, was dismissed. She claimed unfair dismissal. Her employer argued that he had dismissed all those on strike, and was therefore immune from action.

The case went through the whole of the legal process. Eventually after several appeals the House of Lords decided that an employer had to dismiss all striking employees in order to retain immunity from unfair dismissal proceedings. Ms Stock's claim succeeded (*Frank Jones (Tipton) Ltd v Stock*, 1978).

CONDITIONS FOR CLAIMING UNFAIR DISMISSAL

Constructive dismissal
If an employee resigns voluntarily there can be no unfair dismissal unless there is **constructive dismissal**. Constructive or implied dismissal occurs where the employer's conduct is a serious breach of contract entitling the employee to leave without notice.

Minimum qualifying period
The employee must have worked for the employer for at least two years, to be able to bring a case for unfair dismissal. However there are some important exceptions. This qualifying period is *not* required if the dismissal arose from:

- trade union activities
- race discrimination
- sex discrimination

Minimum hours of work
The employee must have been working for at least 16 hours a week unless he had been employed for at least 8 hours a week for five years or more.

Time limit

Claims must be made within 3 months from the date of dismissal, unless the Tribunal can be persuaded to allow a claim out of time. *Note*: this time limit is much shorter than that required for civil actions in the courts (normally six years).

Excluded categories

Employees over retiring age, or ordinarily working abroad, cannot claim unfair dismissal.

CONTINUITY OF EMPLOYMENT

As we have seen, an employee must be able to show that he worked for the employer for at least two years, in order to claim for unfair dismissal. It could therefore be important to show continuity of employment for this qualifying period, because:

- A break in continuity may cause loss of rights.

- The length of continuous employment may affect amounts of compensation, eg when based on redundancy awards.

Continuity continues even though a business is

- taken over
- transferred to an associated employer, which usually means one having substantially the same owners.

What is continuous employment?

The following conditions must be considered:

- The contract of employment must require more than 16 hours per week (or 8 hours or more a week for five years).

- Any gap in continuity must be temporary only.

Factors not breaking continuity

The following will not normally break continuity of employment:

1. Absence through sickness or injury for up to 26 weeks.
2. Absence through pregnancy for up to 26 weeks.

3. Temporary cessation of work.
4. Matters arising by agreement or custom.
5. Re-employment after unfair dismissal.
6. Strikes.

Recent cases on 'continuous employment'

The employee who was transferred
Mr A ran two companies, one a bakery and the other a catering firm.
He held 46% of the shares in the bakery and 99% of the shares in the
catering firm. In reality he controlled both companies. Mr Newbold
was employed by the bakery. After four years he was transferred to
the catering firm. Two years later he was made redundant. His claim
for redundancy payment was based on six years' continuous service.
He argued that his transfer was from one associated employer to
another.

It was held that the transfer had broken Mr Newbold's period of
continuous employment. The employers had not been associated
because the test was one of shareholding control. The majority
required was 51%, which Mr A did not have (*Secretary of State for
Employment v Newbold*, 1981).

A case of last-minute notice of dismissal
Mrs West was one week and one day short of a full year's employment
with Knees Ltd and had therefore not qualified to claim unfair
dismissal (one year had been the required period at the time). Her
employer gave her a week's notice, orally, with the intention that she
should fail by one day to qualify to claim for unfair dismissal. Mrs
West made a claim.

It was held that the notice ran from the day *after* it was given. It
would be an injustice to allow it to run from the day it was given—for
example, notice could be given thirty seconds before the end of the
day's work. Mrs West was therefore qualified to make the claim (*West
v Knees Ltd*, 1986).

DISMISSAL FOR MISCONDUCT

Misconduct is one of the grounds on which an employer can justify a
dismissal as fair. It is of course for the Tribunal to decide whether or
not the actions or omissions amounted to misconduct. There have
been many cases on this question. Here we will see how two of them

were dealt with by the Tribunal; one involved a charge of dishonesty, and the other a question of lack of investigation by the employer.

Cases alleging misconduct

Accused of stealing pork chops
Mrs MacCuish was one of three employees working in the company's store. The manager found two unwrapped packets of pork chops. The two other employees denied knowledge of the chops, and the manager assumed that Mrs MacCuish had taken them illegally. She was accused of stealing the chops and replied that she had intended to pay for them but had forgotten to do so. The manager did not believe this and dismissed her. She claimed that the dismissal had been unfair.

The industrial tribunal decided that there had been an unfair dismissal. The manager should have made inquiries as soon as he found the chops instead of leaping to the conclusion that they had been stolen (*Low & Co Ltd v MacCuish*, 1979).

The employer who failed to investigate properly
Mr Henderson, a coach driver, took a group of schoolchildren on an outing. One of the teachers made verbal complaints against him, followed by a letter. It was alleged that a child had been thrown from her seat during sudden braking and had needed five stitches. After a brief interview, at which Mr Henderson was shown a copy of the letter, he was dismissed. He was not given a chance to study the letter before making a reply. His employer took no steps to interview any of the passengers, nor did they take independent steps to check the complaints.

The tribunal decided that the dismissal was unfair. A proper investigation must be carried out every time (*Henderson v Granville Tours Ltd*, 1982).

DISMISSAL FOR POOR JOB PERFORMANCE

Poor job performance is a common reason for dismissal. But employees have the following important rights in the matter:

- Employees are entitled to a written warning that dismissal will follow if performance does not improve. *Note*: if there is misunderstanding or disagreement as to what constitutes adequate job performance, the employee may be well advised to seek written clarification from the employer.

- Employees are entitled to proper training and information to enable them to discharge their duties adequately.

- Employees should be given a chance to explain poor performance.

Some real life examples

The case of the argumentative manager
Mr Jacomb was a manager. He had arguments with a number of his employer's clients, as a result of which the employer lost contracts. He was dismissed without warning and claimed unfair dismissal.

It was held that, although Mr Jacomb should have been warned, there was no unfair dismissal because he was not capable of changing his ways, even though he knew that his job was at risk (*Dunning Ltd v Jacomb* 1973).

The electrician not wanted by other contractors
Mr Boxall was an electrician. His work was not of a high standard. His employers were told that other contractors did not want Mr Boxall on their sites. He was dismissed without warning. It was held that the dismissal had been unfair because he had never been given any opportunity to explain or chance to improve, his poor performance (*Sutton & Gates Ltd v Boxall*, 1978).

AMOUNT OF AWARD FOR UNFAIR DISMISSAL

Basic award
The award made by a tribunal is normally for whatever sum would have been paid as redundancy payment. It is calculated by reference to gross (not net) weekly pay. It is not normally subject to tax.

Compensatory award
This is assessed as follows:

1. Loss of earnings during the time from dismissal up to the date of hearing, with a further period during which it is reasonable for the claimant to be unemployed.

2. Loss of statutory protection, because it will take another two years for the claimant to gain the right to a redundancy payment. This is usually £100.

3. Loss of pension rights.

4. Expenses incurred in seeking new employment.

5. Loss of right to long notice.

6. Loss of benefit of National Insurance contributions.

Adjustment of award

Reduction
The amount of these awards may be reduced where the employee has contributed to the dismissal by his own behaviour, or has failed to seek new employment, or has received an *ex gratia* payment from the employer.

Increase
Awards may be increased if the employer has failed to comply with a reinstatement or re-engagement order.

5
Redundancy Rights

This chapter deals with the following topics:

- the meaning of redundancy
- the right to union consultation
- the right to fair treatment
- rights on a change of ownership
- offers of new employment
- guarantee payments
- calculation of redundancy payment

MEANING OF REDUNDANCY

Redundancies arise when an employer's requirement for work of a particular kind done by an employee has ceased or diminished, temporarily or permanently.

Sometimes it may not be clear whether an employer's action in altering work arrangements amounts to redundancy or not.

One case involved Lesney, the producers of Matchbox models; they found that they could no longer sustain long production hours in their factory, due to a falling off in trade. In place of a single day shift with overtime, they proposed two day shifts. Under this plan, total hours of work would be reduced, but the number of employees would be maintained and they would continue to do the same type of work. The company said these changes were necessary in the interests of efficiency. An employee refused to accept the changed hours and was dismissed. He claimed a redundancy payment.

The Court of Appeal rejected the claim. The fact that the company was cutting back its production did not mean that there was a redundancy situation (*Lesney Products v Nolan*, 1977).

Notice of Redundancy

Dear Mr X

This is to confirm our discussion with regard to the question of redundancy.

As you are probably aware from that meeting it appears that your redundancy is inevitable.

That being so we intend to follow our customary/agreed redundancy procedure, a copy of which is attached.

As was explained to you, that procedure means that you are entitled to put to management anything which you feel might have a bearing on the matter. That includes any suggestion on your part for any change to the procedure itself.

In particular, if you feel that there is any way by which your redundancy can be avoided or in any way handled differently you are invited to say so now.

We shall ourselves continue to examine the matter and if we find that there is any alternative that is reasonably open to us we shall let you know.

It is with considerable regret that we have to take this course, and we do wish to make sure that all possible avenues are explored. Therefore, anything you wish to put forward at this stage will receive careful consideration.

Yours sincerely

An example of a notice of redundancy.

THE RIGHT TO UNION CONSULTATION

Statutory right to consultation
Under Section 99 of the **Employment Protection Act 1975**, employers
must consult unions about redundancies. This applies to all workers
subject to redundancy, even those with less than two years' service,
and part-timers.

It does not however apply to:

- Crown employees
- short-term workers

What does consultation mean?
Consultation means that the employer must give the following
information to the union:

- the reasons for the proposed redundancies
- the numbers of the proposed redundancies
- the methods for selecting those to be made redundant
- the method of carrying out the redundancies

When must consultation begin?
Consultation must begin at the earliest opportunity. If the rules are
not obeyed by the employer, redundant workers may be entitled to
compensation.

A case of last-minute consultation
An employer had carried on a confectionery business for many years.
It was known that the firm was in serious financial difficulties, but
redundancies were only notified two hours before the final shift, when
the business closed down. The employees claimed compensation. The
employer argued that the special circumstances of the case meant that
it had not needed to consult the union.

It was held that the employer had known of its financial difficulties
long before the business had closed down, and should have consulted
with the unions. Insolvency alone does not amount to a 'special
circumstance' (*Clarks of Hove Ltd v Bakers Union*, 1978).

THE RIGHT TO FAIR TREATMENT

Employees have the right to be treated fairly in the matter of redundancy. What 'fairness' is will depend on the circumstances of each case.

The Williams v Compair Maxam case

In *Williams v Compair Maxam* (1982) the Employment Appeal Tribunal set out the following rules:

1. As much warning as possible must be given to trade unions and employees of impending redundancies.

   (a) The employer should consult with the trade unions about how its desired objectives can be met with as little hardship as possible.

   (b) Part of this consultation process should be directed towards setting criteria for individual selections for redundancy.

2. These criteria should be applied in an objective way, not depending on the sole discretion of one person.

3. The employer should ensure that selections are made according to the criteria, and should consider any representations from the union.

4. Any opportunity of offering alternative employment should be closely investigated.

The facts of the Compair Maxam case were that selection should be made on the basis that those retained would be those most likely to keep the company viable. None of the principles had been applied, and the selections were held to be unfair.

The case of the redundant van driver

The following illustrates the principle of fairness.

Mr Polkey was a van driver. Due to mounting financial losses the company decided to replace its drivers with driver salesmen. Mr Polkey was told that he was being made redundant and was driven home immediately by one of the other drivers, who was himself made redundant on his return to work. Mr Polkey claimed compensation for unfair dismissal on the basis that he had not been warned about the impending redundancy.

This case went through the whole tribunal and court procedure: from industrial tribunal to EAT to Court of Appeal to House of Lords. The eventual decision was that the tribunal must look at the question whether the employer had acted **reasonably**. It was not correct to look at the question whether the employer's behaviour would have made any difference (*Polkey v Edmund Walker (Holdings) Ltd*, 1987).

TRANSFER OF OWNERSHIP OF A BUSINESS

Problems can sometimes arise when ownership of a business is transferred. The new owners may be keen to reduce their overhead and labour costs; the old owners may be unwilling to do much to help employees for whom they no longer feel responsibility. But an important general rule applies:

- Where a business is sold or transferred as a going concern, the general rule is that the rights and duties of employers and employees are also transferred.

Dismissals occurring by reason of the transfer will therefore normally be regarded as unfair. However, the law in this area is difficult and complex: professional advice should be sought. The following case histories illustrate problems which may arise in this situation.

Cases regarding transfer of ownership

When is a transfer not a transfer?
Total Oil negotiated to buy a filling station from Premier Motors. Two employees worked for Premier Motors. Total Oil clearly stated its wish from the outset not to continue the employment of these employees. The sale was concluded. In the same legal transaction, the business was licensed back to Premier Motors. This was intended as a short-term measure only until new licensees could be found. When new licensees were found the two employees' employment came to an end. An industrial tribunal held that the liability to pay a redundancy payment fell on Premier Motors and not on Total Oil. Premier Motors appealed.

The EAT ruled that the liability for redundancy payments fell on Total Oil. The transfer was a transfer of a business as a going concern. The Transfer of Undertakings Regulations 1981 therefore applied.

The fact that Total Oil had all along declined to take the two employees into their own employment made no difference. The effect of the Regulations was to carry over the employment from the transferor (Premier) to the transferee (Total), regardless of the wishes of either party. The refusal by Total to continue this employment amounted to a dismissal of the employees. Under the Regulations this dismissal was treated as a dismissal for redundancy. Therefore the liability to make redundancy payments fell on Total. This was the case even though Total had immediately licensed the business to another party (in this case Premier): for a moment, however brief, Total had been legal owner. At this moment the legal obligation to meet redundancy liabilities became fixed on them (*Premier Motors (Medway) Ltd v Total Oil Great Britain*, 1983).

A Truly Fair transfer?
Truly Fair Ltd sold one of their children's wear factories to a company which planned to use it to make men's trousers. Ms Crompton's contract was taken up by the new company. She continued her job as a machinist using exactly the same machine. For her, the only difference was that she made men's trousers instead of children's wear. In order to safeguard her position she made a redundancy claim against Truly Fair.

Her claim succeeded. There had been no 'transfer' of a business. The new owners had not bought a going concern but merely a collection of assets which they wished to put to their own use. (*Crompton v Truly Fair Ltd*, 1965).

OFFER OF NEW EMPLOYMENT

An employee who qualifies for a redundancy payment may lose entitlement if he or she unreasonably refuses an offer of:

- Re-employment on the same terms as the old employment
- Suitable employment where the terms are different

Specimen offer of re-employment
Here is a specimen offer of re-employment under a new contract made to a redundant employee:

Dear Mr X

In view of our recent discussion about your dismissal on the grounds of redundancy, I am pleased to be able to make the following offer:

We would propose to re-employ you as an Office Junior on terms and conditions to be separately communicated to you. Please let me know whether you would be prepared to discuss this proposal further.

Yours faithfully

The case of a decision regretted
Mr Hindes agreed to try out a completely different job in a new factory, in worse environmental conditions (it was much hotter and smelled of paint) at £10 per week less than he earned in his previous job. After seven days working in the new job he brought the trial to an end and claimed a redundancy payment.

The Industrial Tribunal held that, as Mr Hindes did not seem to object to the drop in pay and had said he liked the new job, it was suitable to him and he had brought it to an end unreasonably. Mr Hindes appealed.

His appeal was successful. An offer of employment was only suitable if it was of reasonably equivalent employment. Mr Hindes was only prepared to accept the drop in pay if the other aspects of the job were to his liking. When he decided he did not like the job itself, his reservation about the pay re-emerged to make the job offer unsuitable (*Hindes v Superfine Ltd*, 1979).

Right to a trial period of new employment
If an employee is offered a suitable new job on different terms from his old one, he is entitled to a trial period in the new job.

The trial period in the basement
Air Canada's lease on their Dover Street premises ran out. They moved the staff to another office site. The result was that Mrs Lee's job as telephone operator moved from a relatively comfortable third floor position to a rather dark (as she regarded it) basement. Her contract said nothing about a liability to be moved. Consequently her employer's insistence on the move was in breach of her contract. Nevertheless, she agreed to try out the new location. After two months she had had enough and resigned.

The industrial tribunal had found Mrs Lee unfairly dismissed. In fact she was redundant. Although Air Canada had not expressly dismissed Mrs Lee by notice, she was, in fact, constructively dismissed. Even though she had worked for two months in her new job she had not necessarily accepted it. When an employer imposes new terms of employment which technically amount to a breach of contract, the employee has a reasonable time to consider his or her reaction to the new arrangements. So long as the employee reaches a decision that he or she does not like the new arrangements before a 'reasonable' period expires, he or she can leave and claim redundancy. Alternatively, by conduct or words the employee might show that he or she has accepted the new job, in which case the 'contractual' trial period then comes to an end (*Air Canada v Lee*, 1978).

GUARANTEE PAYMENTS

Employees may be entitled to guarantee payments by their employer where there is a **lay-off** caused by a reduction in the workload. The conditions for such payments to be made are:

- A complete day or days' loss of work.

- Employees must have complied with reasonable requirements to ensure availability of their services.

- Any offer of suitable alternative work must not have been unreasonably refused.

- There must not have been any industrial action.

Failure by an employer to make such payment may lead to a complaint to an industrial tribunal.

HOW TO CALCULATE A REDUNDANCY PAYMENT

1. *Calculate a week's pay*
   A week's pay is the amount payable for a week's work under the contract of employment. Where the normal working hours do not vary, this poses no problem. Complications arise in the case of overtime, piece-work or varying shift systems. The maximum for a week's pay, with effect from April 1st 1990, is £184.

2. *Apply the multiplier*
   The amount of a week's pay is multiplied by a multiplier depending on age, as follows:

1 ½ for every year during the whole of which the employee was aged 41 or over.

1 for every year during the whole of which the employee was aged between 22 and 40

½ for every year between 18 and 21.

The maximum payable is thus 30 weeks.

Note: some employers operate severance payment schemes which could be more generous than the above.

What if the employer cannot pay?
If the employer has cash flow problems so serious that making redundancy payments would put the business at risk, arrangements can be made for the employee to be paid direct from the **Redundancy Fund**.

If the employer is insolvent (its liabilities exceed its assets) any redundancy payments due will be paid by the Department of Employment (which will seek to recover the debt from the assets of the business).

6
Your Trade Union Rights

This chapter covers the following topics:

- legal status of unions
- belonging to a union
- union rule books
- industrial action

LEGAL STATUS OF UNIONS

A trade union has a legal status somewhere between a company and a club. This has the following consequences:

1. It can make contracts, for example to buy and sell goods, own or rent property, employ staff, borrow and lend money, and so on.

2. Its property must be held by trustees.

3. It can sue or be sued (except in some cases of trade disputes), in the civil courts, for example for breach of contract, negligence or defamation.

4. It can be liable for crimes. This means that it can be fined, and its officers fined or imprisoned if found guilty of criminal acts.

5. It may be recognised by employers for negotiating purposes.

Recognition of unions
In smaller businesses fewer staff belong to a union. However, if several employees decide to join a union they may ask the firm to recognise it.

There is no statutory obligation to recognise a union. In making the decision the firm will weigh up the pros and cons according to the

Part of a typical union recognition agreement.

situation. The union may then represent individuals in presenting
grievances and in disciplinary action. They do not, in this case, have
rights to negotiate terms and conditions of employment for the
employees. If there is enough employee support for the union, full
recognition may follow, provided the employer consents.

An example of a typical union recognition agreement is shown
above.

The SOGAT case of 1987
The legal position and status of a union was well illustrated in the case
of SOGAT, the print union, in 1987, when it came into conflict with
Rupert Murdoch's News Group over the move of the company from
its old London headquarters to a new high-tech base at Wapping.

NGN dismissed a large number of its employees, members of
SOGAT, and moved to Wapping. SOGAT organised pickets, marches

and rallies against NGN. NGN asked the High Court for injunctions restraining SOGAT from carrying out unlawful acts.

The decision of the court was that SOGAT branches were trade unions liable to be sued in their own name, and had been responsible for unlawful actions including obstructing the highway. The injunctions were granted (*News Group Newspapers v SOGAT*, 1989).

BELONGING TO A UNION

Your right to belong to a union
An employee can complain to an industrial tribunal if he has been dismissed for becoming a trade union member, or for trade union activities. An employer has a duty not to prevent or deter an employee from joining a union.

Your right not to belong to a union
Since the introduction of the **Employment Act 1980**, employees may not be dismissed or chosen for redundancy for **not** belonging to a union. Union dues or charitable alternatives cannot be deducted from your pay without your consent.

What is a closed shop?
This is an agreement under which employees are obliged to become members of a union and therefore subject to its rules. A closed shop agreement may be informal, arising from custom and practice. In general, such agreements to be binding must now be approved by 85% of those voting in a secret ballot. Employees may refuse to be part of closed shop arrangements on the grounds of conscience or deeply held personal conviction.

Can I have time off for union activities?
Trade union officials may take time off during working hours to carry out union duties or for industrial relations training. It is advisable for employees to reach agreement with employers on the way in which time off is dealt with, for example as to:

- amount and frequency of absences
- any notice required of such absences
- pay for periods of absence
- agreement as to what is meant by 'union duties'

The case of a dismissed shop steward
Mr Shaw had been nominated as an AUEW shop steward for his employer's maintenance department. He approached the employer in connection with a fitter's wages. The employer refused to accept Mr Shaw as a shop steward. A dispute developed and other workers stopped work for one hour as a protest.

As a result of this, Mr Shaw was dismissed. He claimed unfair dismissal compensation on the ground that the reason for his dismissal had been trade union activity. The employer argued that Mr Shaw's activities had amounted to gross misconduct, and had not taken place 'at an appropriate time'.

The case went to the Court of Appeal, which decided as follows:

- Mr Shaw's activities were trade union activities.

- They had not taken place at an appropriate time.

- The problem was not so urgent as to warrant a stoppage of work.

- The employer had not consented to the activities taking place during working hours.

(*Marley Tile Co Ltd v Shaw*, 1980).

UNION RULE BOOKS
Trade union rule books govern relations between members and the union, and its control by officers of the union.

The interpretation of the rules can obviously be a very important matter. A union may find it necessary or desirable to alter its rules from time to time. But whatever a rule book contains, it is subject to the general laws of the land. In particular:

- The discrimination laws apply, so that for example a rule book may not discriminate on grounds of sex or race.

- The rules must not be illegal. For example they must not incite or require people to break the law.

- Special laws apply to political funds, amalgamation of unions and the way strike ballots are conducted.

OBJECTS CLAUSE

1 Principal objects

The principal objects of the union are to regulate the relations between workers [employed in (*name industries or businesses in which membership are employed)* and such other industries as the executive committee may from time to time determine appropriate *or* employed as (*give job description of membership*)] and employers or employers' associations.

2 Subsidiary objects

The subsidiary objects of the union shall be:

2.1   to protect and promote the interests of its members

2.2   to assist and enable its members to obtain fair remuneration for their labour and the establishment and maintenance of satisfactory conditions of employment

2.3   to negotiate and promote the settlement of disputes arising between its members and employers or employers' associations and between its members [by conciliation or arbitration]

2.4   to provide financial or other assistance at the discretion of the executive committee to a member or where appropriate the member's dependants in respect of any matter arising out of:

    2.4:1 the sickness of the member

    2.4:2 an injury to the member sustained during the course of the member's employment

    2.4:3 the death of the member

    2.4:4 the unemployment of the member (through proper causes)

    2.4:5 any matter appertaining to the employment of the member

2.5   to provide for legal or other assistance to its members who are dismissed from their employment

2.6   to provide legal or other assistance to its members where (in the opinion of the executive committee) necessary [or expedient] in matters concerning the employment of members or for securing compensation for members who suffer injury by accident in the course of their employment or travelling to and from work

2.7   subject to the provision of the Trade Union Act 1913 (as amended) to engage in all political objects

2.8   to assist in securing the introduction of new legislation and in securing a more efficient application of existing legislation which may affect the general and material welfare of its members

2.9   to purchase or by any other means acquire and take options over any property whatever and any rights or privileges of any kind over or in respect of any property

2.10 to sell improve manage prepare develop lease mortgage dispose of turn to account or otherwise deal with all or any part of the property and rights of the union

2.11 to invest and deal with the money of the union not immediately required in such manner as from time to time may be determined and to hold or otherwise deal with any investments made

2.12 to borrow and raise money in any manner and to secure the repayment of any money borrowed raised or owing in such manner as may be determined by the executive committee...

An extract from some typical trade union rules.

- The results of union elections may be reviewed and set aside by the courts. This might happen for example if a union officer or member has grounds for believing the results of an election to have been rigged in some way.

- The principles of natural justice apply. In other words union rules should not breach any fundamental idea of fairness.

An example of a rule book dispute

A few years ago the executive council of the National Union of Seamen decided to levy money from its members to support the National Union of Mineworkers. A member of the NUS asked the High Court to declare that the levy was invalid because only a general meeting of the union had power to do so, under the union's rules. In 1985 the court decided that the action of the executive council was null and void because it had not been within the union rules (*Hopkins v National Union of Seamen*, 1985).

INDUSTRIAL ACTION

The term industrial action is not a legal expression as such. It is a general term which can for example mean all or any of the following:

- Stopping work: going on **strike**.

- Having a **go slow** or **working to rule**, when the employees refuse to do anything not specifically required by their agreement with the employer.

- **Picketing**, which means standing or demonstrating outside the workplace. Primary picketing refers to picketing at the employees' own workplace; secondary picketing means picketing at the workplace of other employees who are not directly involved.

There is no legal right to strike which expressly exists in English law. The basic position is that if an employee stops work or otherwise fails to carry out his obligations under his contract of employment, the employer is entitled to stop payment of wages or salary. Beyond this basic point about breach of the employment contract, there are a number of other consequences of going on strike, arising for example out of employment law or the criminal law.

Consequences of going on strike
Strikes may have the following consequences for employees and their unions:

Welfare benefits
Social security benefits are withheld.

Dismissal
Employers would be entitled to dismiss striking employees for breach of contract.

Pay
There is no right to pay during a strike.

Secondary action
Secondary picketing or other action to bring pressure on a party not in the dispute is generally unlawful.

Union liability
Trade unions themselves are *not* liable for damages for breach of contract which takes place 'in contemplation or furtherance of a trade dispute'.

Criminal offices
Various criminal offences may arise, for example **intimidation** (a threat of violence) or **conspiracy** (an agreement to break the law). Suspected persons may be arrested by the police and brought before a magistrates court.

Strike ballots
Under the Trade Union Act 1984, industrial action must be approved by a specially held ballot. The Act sets out detailed rules for the holding of such ballots.

Court injunctions
Employers may apply for **injunctions** to restrain unlawful acts. When the court issues an injunction, failure to obey it may result in fines or imprisonment for **contempt of court** or **sequestration** (which operates by taking over all the property of a union).

Picketing
This method of enforcing strike action by standing outside the

workplace has led to prosecutions for the following:

Obstructing the highway
Obstructing the police
Assaults
Affray and riot

The case of the dismissed coach driver
Mr Winnett's coach driver colleagues regarded him as their
representative, although he was not a shop steward in the formal
sense. A pay dispute arose. The company had a procedure by which
two days' notice in writing had to be given before the drivers could be
called together for a meeting. When the company insisted on this, the
drivers stopped work. Mr Winnett stated that he would join this
action. He was dismissed.

His claim for unfair dismissal was not allowed, despite his
argument that the reason for his dismissal had been trade union
activity. The Employment Appeal Tribunal decided that he had been
dismissed for being on strike (*Winnett v Seamarks Brothers Ltd*,
1978).

Selective sacking and unfair dismissal
The general rule is that industrial action amounts to a breach of the
contract of employment. There is nothing to stop an employer
dismissing all those taking part in such action, but selective sacking of
some strikers may amount to unfair dismissal.

Mr Winnett's colleagues were already on strike over the dismissal
of another employee. He was between shifts, and his employer asked
him if he was going to come in for his shift. He said he would not, and
was dismissed. He argued that he had been dismissed for taking part
in trade union activity.

The court decided that, in legal terms, Mr Winnett's part in the
strike began from the moment he declared his intention not to come
in for this next shift. He had been dismissed for taking part in the
strike (*Winnett v Seamarks Brothers Ltd, 1978*).

What happens if someone is frightened into strike action?
This question arose in a firm called Modern Methods and Materials
Ltd. The company had already closed down one plant. But further
savings were needed. Redundancies were in the air.

A meeting of employees was called at the factory gates first thing in the morning. The purpose of the meeting was to discuss industrial action. As employees arrived they were encouraged to join the meeting and vociferously discouraged from going in to work. One woman who did go in to work was abused and called a 'scab'. Another woman, a Mrs Leith, intended to go into work but, in fear of abuse, joined the meeting for a short time before going home.

Those employees who actively attended the meeting were dismissed, but Mrs Leith was allowed to return to work. Two of the dismissed strikers claimed that their dismissal was unfair. They argued that Mrs Leith was to be treated as 'taking part in a strike or other industrial action' despite her disagreement with the strike. They said that her physical attendance at the meeting was what counted, not her personal feelings or motives.

The Court of Appeal agreed that Mrs Leith had taken part in the strike. Her own dissent from the action was immaterial. In industrial action people are to be judged by their outward deeds and not their inner intentions. The simple fact of an employee's voluntary absence from work during a strike meant that she was taking part in it (*Coates and Venables v Modern Methods and Materials Ltd*, 1982).

Do employees risk their jobs just by threatening strike action?

This question arose a few years ago at a company called Midlands Plastics Ltd. Wage negotiations had failed to produce a satisfactory settlement. The works committee delivered a letter to the managing director which threatened that if wage demands were not met in full then it was the workers' intention to take industrial action.

The employees were all dismissed, and claimed unfair dismissal. The employers argued that industrial action had already begun and that the tribunal could not hear the claims. The tribunal decided however that the threat to take industrial action does not in itself amount to industrial action (*Midlands Plastics Ltd v Till, 1983*).

7
Your Rights to Equality at Work

This chapter deals with the following subjects:

- Sex discrimination
- Race discrimination
- Genuine occupational qualification
- The right to equal pay
- Maternity rights
- Disabled persons
- Past offenders
- How to obtain remedies

EQUALITY AT WORK

The last twenty years or so have seen important pieces of legislation intended to provide fairer and more equal treatment of people at work, whether they are male or female or members of an ethnic minority. The key pieces of legislation have been as follows.

- The Equal Pay Act 1970
- The Sex Discrimination Acts 1975 and 1986
- The Race Relations Act 1976
- The Rehabilitation of Offenders Act 1974

Codes of Practice
Codes of practice explaining in detail how to avoid discrimination in employment are available from the **Commission for Racial Equality** and the **Equal Opportunities Commission.**

Commission for Racial Equality
Elliot House
10/12 Allington Street
London SW1E 5EH
Tel: (071) 828 7022

Equal Opportunities Commission
Overseas House
Quay Street
Manchester M3 3HN
Tel: (061) 833 9244

Direct and indirect discrimination
Discrimination may be direct or indirect:

- **Direct discrimination** occurs in relation to the offer of employment or its terms.

- **Indirect discrimination** applies where a requirement is applied so that the proportion of women or persons of a racial group who can comply with that requirement is considerably smaller than the proportion of men or other racial groups who can comply.

The rights of job applicants
The legislation concerning discrimination applies not just to those already employed: job applicants too are entitled to the protection of the law.

Employers are under a legal obligation not to **discriminate** between applicants with different race, sex or marital status. Some employers have tried to get around these laws by various means—such as excluding ethnic applicants by demanding a higher standard of spoken or written English than is required to do the job well. Such attempts are clearly discriminatory.

Applicants who feel that they have been discriminated against are entitled to take their case to an Industrial Tribunal.

- Advertisements must not be written in a way that may be considered discriminatory, eg by the use of 'he' throughout, or expressions such as 'Girl Friday'.

- When it comes to the interview, applicants are entitled to be given a similar format for the interview—for instance, by having an employee specification as the framework. Applicants are entitled to be asked broadly the same questions.

- Female applicants may be discriminated against by questions such as – 'When are you going to get married?' 'When are you going to have children?' or 'What arrangements have you made for child care while you are at work?' Male applicants are not normally asked these questions.

- Applicants belonging to an ethnic minority are entitled not to be asked questions about their racial or ethnic background which would not be asked of white applicants.

There are no very hard-and-fast rules about this. The legislation has enacted the general principles, and it is a matter for the tribunals to adjudicate on the circumstances of particular cases. The following case illustrates the law in action.

'Wanted – typist'

A firm of solicitors rejected Miss James, a coloured woman, for a job. She had typing speeds of 80 wpm and was amply qualified for the job. The company had declared that no experience was necessary.

To her surprise the job was readvertised and she reapplied. The same partner who had interviewed her previously did not ask her to sit down and said he saw no point in interviewing her. She had a hostile discussion with him.

The job was given to a white girl with shorthand speeds of only 35 wpm. It was claimed that the interviewer told the successful applicant that he liked her name as it was a nice English name and told her that he couldn't understand why an English employer would want to take on a coloured girl when English girls were available.

The solicitors said they had not selected Miss James for a variety of reasons, including the fact that she had been unemployed for the previous three years. The industrial tribunal said that Mr X, the interviewer, might not have been motivated totally by racial considerations; however, they *were* an important factor and they accepted Miss James's claim for damages for racial discrimination. The case came to the Court of Appeal when the firm appealed and the Court of Appeal agreed with the industrial tribunal's view of the law, agreeing that race had to be an important factor rather than the sole factor (*Owen & Briggs v James*, 1982).

SEX DISCRIMINATION

The Equal Pay Act 1970

Under this Act men and women, working full or part-time, are entitled to equal treatment in their terms and conditions of employment where they are employed to do the same or similar work, or alternatively work of equal value.

The Sex Discrimination Acts 1975 and 1986

It is unlawful to discriminate on the grounds of sex, in the recruitment of staff, the terms of full or part-time employment, in training or promotion.

Discrimination against a woman occurs where, on the grounds of her sex, she is treated less favourably than a man. Both direct and indirect discrimination are unlawful.

The Act protects men as well as women.

An employer may not discriminate against people on the grounds of their marital status.

Sexual harassment

Sexual harassment can be a source of much irritation, anger and misery in the workplace, and anyone—female or male—suffering from unwelcome sexual attentions is entitled to the protection of the law. The criminal law covering the field of 'offences against the person' deals with the most serious forms of sexual misconduct such as indecent assault or rape. An employee committing such acts would certainly be liable to instant dismissal for gross misconduct.

The term sexual harassment however is generally used to refer to misconduct of a less serious nature; whether or not there is any criminal act, the victim is entitled to the protection of the sex discrimination laws. The following two examples illustrate what may occur.

The victim who requested a job transfer

Two male colleagues of Mrs Porcelli subjected her to sexual harassment by comparing her physique to that of pictures in the press, by handing her phallic objects and by asking her if she needed a screw. She requested a transfer to another job and claimed sex discrimination. It was held that the acts of harassment resulting in the 'detriment' of having to find another job amounted to unlawful sex discrimination under the Act of 1975 (*Porcelli v Strathclyde Regional Council*, 1984).

A case of sexual provocation

Mrs Wileman was sexually harassed by a director of her employers' firm, for a period of four-and-a-half years. Her complaint for sex discrimination was accepted, but she was awarded only £50 damages because she had worn 'scanty and provocative' clothes to work (*Wileman v Minilec Ltd*, 1988).

Discrimination against men

While the legislation was introduced mainly as a means of improving the position of women at work, men are equally entitled to the protection of the same law. For example, a case involving the Ministry of Defence illustrated that men could not be made to do work which they had as good a reason as women to refuse to undertake.

Mr X worked in a munitions factory. 'Colour bursting' shells which were used in target practice were made, as well as other types of ammunition. These shells gave off red or orange colour when they exploded, a colour made from red or orange dye.

Nobody liked working in the 'colour-bursting' shop, so the Ministry of Defence had a system whereby anyone who wanted to do overtime had to do a stint in the colour bursting shop. However, this condition applied only to men, and not women. Women were excused on the grounds that the dye would ruin their hair, and they objected to using the communal showers.

Mr X complained that he was discriminated against on grounds of his sex because of this one-sided condition about overtime work.

It was found by the Court of Appeal that the condition was a **detriment** and that being on grounds of sex (by way of **direct discrimination**) it was unlawful. Mr X had a right not to be discriminated against in this way. The fact that the men were paid extra for working in the 'colour bursting' shop did not offset the unlawfulness of the discrimination. The judge said that 'An employer cannot buy the right to discriminate by making an extra payment' (*Jeremiah v Ministry of Defence*, 1979).

Discrimination as to retirement age
The widely recognised retirement ages are 60 for women and 65 for men. However under the Sex Discrimination Act women who wish to work up until 65 may do so, if that is the retirement age for men in the same company. Employers can no longer set different retirement ages for men and women.

A woman still has a right to a state or occupational pension if she wishes to retire at 60.

RACIAL DISCRIMINATION

The provisions against racial discrimination operate in much the same way as those against sex discrimination. The key piece of legislation is the Race Relations Act of 1976.

The Race Relations Act 1976
No employer, regardless of the numbers they employ, may

discriminate on racial grounds. Employers are also liable for an employee's discrimination if it occurs at work.

An employer must not discriminate in selection procedures, or use unreasonable selection tests which could amount to indirect discrimination.

The failure to offer a job, on grounds of race alone, would clearly be racial discrimination. Existing employees must not be discriminated against in the terms of their employment, promotion, training or any other benefit. An employer may not dismiss, or impose any other penalty on racial grounds.

Evidence of racial discrimination

As with sex discrimination it can be difficult to produce hard evidence of racial discrimination. However, in the absence of positive evidence, where the primary facts indicate discrimination and a difference of race, the employer will be called upon to give an explanation. If this is inadequate or patently unsatisfactory or untrue, it is open to draw the inference that the discrimination was on racial grounds.

A recent case involving the North West Thames Regional Health Authority illustrates this principle.

Racial discrimination against a microbiologist

Dr X applied for a post as a consultant microbiologist and was interviewed by the Advisory Appointments Committee, which made subjective assessments of candidates. When Dr X was not appointed she complained that it was on grounds of her race. Her claim was upheld by an industrial tribunal who found that the interview was 'little more than a sham', that the decisions were made on a basis amounting almost to arbitrariness, and that the successful candidate had less qualifications and experience than Dr X.

However, when the employers appealed the EAT held that the tribunal had erred in fact. Although the successful candidate was white and less suitable and Dr X was unfairly and wrongly not chosen, the tribunal was not entitled to conclude that the discrimination could *only* be attributed to the difference of race (*North West Thames Regional Health Authority v Noone*, 1987).

Employer's vicarious liability for racial discrimination

We have already considered the question of employers' vicarious liability for the conduct of their employees (page 19). An employer could in principle be vicariously liable for racial discrimination carried out by an employee. The Post Office was sued for this reason a few years ago.

The case of the racialist postman
Mr and Mrs X, who were both black and of Jamaican origin, lived next door to a postman. The postman saw an envelope addressed to them while he was sorting the mail and wrote on the back of it 'Go back to Jamaica Sambo'. He also added a cartoon of a smiling mouth and eyes. When the letter was delivered to Mr and Mrs X they brought proceedings against the Post Office, seeking a declaration that the Post Office had discriminated against them, asking for an injunction to prevent further discrimination and claiming damages. When their claim was dismissed on the basis that the postman had not acted in the course of his employment, they appealed to the Court of Appeal.

The higher court held that the Post Office was *not* vicariously liable, as the postman's act was not authorised by them. It was purely an act of personal malevolence and could not be regarded as an unauthorised way of performing the duties for which he was employed (*Irving and Irving v The Post Office*, 1987).

Racially offensive language at work
The use of racially offensive language by one employee to another will not make the employer liable for race discrimination unless the victim also suffers some further detriment as a result of the co-employee's action. Racially abusive language is not by itself a **detriment** as defined by the Race Relations Act 1976.

An insult but no 'detriment'
When Mrs Y, a coloured secretary, overheard one of the managers say 'get this typing done by the wog', she submitted a claim for compensation for race discrimination. However, it was held that a claim could not be made unless the employee could demonstrate some concrete disadvantage arising, such as refusal of promotion. Although the words were aimed at Mrs Y and were discriminatory in the ordinary sense of the word, the 1976 Act requires that the claimant suffer a **detriment** before a claim for compensation can be made (*De Souza v Automobile Association*, 1985).

GENUINE OCCUPATIONAL QUALIFICATION (GOQ)

There is one major exception to the laws against discrimination at work, and that is **genuine occupational qualification**. This means that it is lawful to employ people of a particular racial or sexual group for particular purposes.

Limitation of GOQ

- GOQ applies only to recruitment, transfer, training and promotion.
- GOQ cannot be used in relation to married persons.

Examples of possible GOQs

1. those involving the body, such as modelling;
2. those involving entertainment, such as acting, dancing or singing;
3. those involving questions of decency and privacy, such as sanitary facilities;
4. those connected with single-sex establishments such as prisons;
5. those subject to legal restrictions, such as night work in factories.

The man who was refused night work with women
The idea of genuine occupational qualification is illustrated by the case of *Sisley v Britannia Security Systems Ltd* (1983). The employer operated a twelve hour shift system, with rest facilities provided on site. Employees undressed and slept during their rest period. Only women were employed on the basis that this would preserve decency. Mr Sisley was rejected for such work and made a claim for compensation under the Act of 1975. It was held that the GOQ exception applied, on the grounds of decency, so Mr Sisley's claim failed.

THE RIGHT TO EQUAL PAY

The aim of the Equal Pay legislation is to ensure that employees do not suffer sex discrimination in relation to pay. Employees must be doing

- similar jobs
- at the same workplace
- for the same employer

before the legislation can apply. Where the work of a woman has been declared equivalent to that of a man under a **job evaluation scheme**, then the woman is entitled to the same pay and terms of employment.

The case of the speech therapist
Dr Enderby, a female speech therapist, was paid less than pharmacists and clinical psychologists. She claimed for equal pay on the basis that speech therapists, being predominantly female, were paid less than predominantly male pharmacists and clinical psychologists. It was assumed that the work of speech therapists was of equal value.

At the hearing it was held that there was no sex discrimination. The different salaries had been agreed through collective bargaining and access to both groups was available to both males and females. There was no less favourable treatment because of sex (*Enderby v Frenchay Health Authority*, 1991).

MATERNITY RIGHTS

The law protects pregnant women at work, entitles them to pay, and in some cases gives them the right to return to work.

Summary of maternity rights
Employees with **more than two years' continuous service** with the company may have:

- the right to return (with exceptions);
- the right to **statutory maternity pay** (SMP);
- the right not to be dismissed by reason of pregnancy;
- the right to paid time off for ante-natal care from a doctor, midwife or health worker. (You are advised to obtain evidence of these appointments which you can produce if necessary to your employer.)

Your right to return
If, immediately before your maternity leave begins your employer has fewer than five employees, failure to permit you to return to your job after maternity leave will not be classed as a dismissal. The law recognises that for small businesses the inconvenience of keeping a job open for the length of maternity leave would be quite great. Larger companies often appoint temporary staff to fill the gap.

To have the right to return you must have had at least two years' continuous service in your company, working more than sixteen hours per week. If you work fewer than sixteen hours, but at least eight hours per week, you must have worked for your employer continuously for at least five years to have the right to return.

You must give written notice of maternity leave
You must inform your employer in writing, at least twenty-one days before the leave commences, that:

- you will be absent due to maternity;
- you intend to return to work after maternity leave;
- the date your baby is due to be born.

For entitlement to return you may leave at any time after the beginning of the eleventh week before your baby is due. You may return to work at any time you wish before the end of the twenty-ninth week after your baby is born. This may be postponed for up to four weeks if you can supply a doctor's certificate.

If your employer contacts you after the birth
Your employer may write to you seven weeks or more after your baby is born, to ask you to decide whether or not you wish to exercise your right to return. If you wish to exercise your right to return, you should reply, in writing, within 14 days of receiving the letter.

Your right to Statutory Maternity Pay

Statutory Maternity Pay (SMP) means pay that you are legally entitled to receive in respect of maternity leave. It is paid by your employer, not for example by the Department of Social Security or Department of Employment. There are two rates of Statutory Maternity Pay, the higher rate and the lower rate. Which is to be paid depends upon the employee's length of service.

How do I qualify for the higher rate?
To qualify for the **higher rate** of SMP you must:

- Have been *employed continuously* by your employer for two years for sixteen or more hours per week (or five years if working between eight and sixteen hours per week) by the time you reach fifteen weeks before the baby is due to be born. This fifteenth week is known as the 'qualifying week'.

- Still be **pregnant eleven weeks** before the baby is due—or have had the baby by that time. That is to say you have not miscarried or had a still birth by that time.

- Have **ceased work** due to pregnancy.

- Have received **medical evidence** that you are pregnant. You will be given a photocopy of form *MAT B1* by the midwife or doctor, showing the date on which the baby is expected.

- Give **21 days' notice in writing** that you will be leaving due to maternity. This applies even if you do not wish to return to work, or do not have the right to return.

- Have average earnings high enough for you to pay **national insurance contributions**.

If you meet all these conditions you are entitled to maternity pay for a total of eighteen weeks, as long as you have given up work by the sixth week before the baby is due. Maternity payments cannot start until the eleventh week before the baby is born.

The higher rate of SMP is paid for the first six weeks of this eighteen week period. This rate is nine-tenths of your average weekly earnings over the eight weeks which end on the pay day immediately before the end of the 'qualifying week'.

During the remaining twelve weeks of maternity pay you will be paid SMP at the lower rate. The amount of this is reviewed annually.

What is the lower rate?
The lower rate of SMP is payable to employees, irrespective of the number of hours they work, with over six months' but under two years' continuous service at the fifteenth week before the baby is due. Otherwise the same rules apply to qualify for this rate as for the higher rate.

Full details about SMP are given in the DSS booklet *Employer's Guide to Statutory Maternity Pay*, and Employment Department booklet PL710, *Employment Rights for the Expectant Mother*.

Maternity rights and the European Court
It is unclear whether English courts are directly bound by decisions of the European Court. However, English courts are certainly obliged to

take notice of such decisions. It is interesting to look at cases brought by a Dutch teacher, and a Danish cashier, which concerned pregnant workers, both of which came before the European Court in 1990.

The case of the pregnant Dutch teacher

Mrs Dekker, a Dutch person, applied for a teaching post. She informed the employer that she was three months pregnant. She was told that her application had been rejected because of her pregnancy. The Dutch courts refused her application for damages, and she appealed to the European Court. The Court held that since only a woman could be refused employment on the ground of pregnancy, such a refusal amounted to direct discrimination based on sex. This could not be justified on the basis that an employer might suffer financial loss by having to give maternity leave (*Dekker, European Court*, 1990).

The case of the pregnant Danish cashier

Mrs H, a Danish person, was employed as a part-time cashier. She became pregnant, and as a consequence of the birth of her child took over 100 days sick leave. The employer dismissed her because of her repeated absences from work. Her action in the Danish courts was dismissed and she appealed to the European Court.

The Court held that the dismissal of a woman on the ground of repeated absences from work through sickness does not amount to sex discrimination if such absences would lead to the dismissal of a man in the same circumstances.

DISABLED PERSONS

The **Disabled Persons (Employment) Acts** 1944 and 1958 state that employers with more than 20 regular workers must employ a quota of registered disabled workers. This is generally 3 per cent. Failure to do so can result in a fine, but prosecutions are very rare.

PAST OFFENDERS

In 1974 Parliament passed the **Rehabilitation of Offenders Act**, designed to make it easier for past offenders to obtain a job and establish themselves in normal society.

- A person with a minor conviction may treat it as if it never happened, if after a period of rehabilitation, no further serious offence has been committed. The conviction is then said to be 'spent'.

An employer may ask a job applicant whether he has a conviction but the candidate is not obliged to admit to a spent conviction. Employers may not ask if the applicant has a spent conviction.

It is unlawful for an employer to discriminate against an employee with a spent conviction. Nor may the employee be dismissed for that reason.

The period of rehabilitation before a conviction becomes spent varies with the length of the sentence. Sentences of over two and half years do not become spent.

HOW TO OBTAIN REMEDIES

Initial advice
The Equal Opportunities Commission and the Commission for Racial Equality give advice on discrimination to both employers and employees. These bodies may issue **non-discrimination notices**.

Is there a deadline for complaints?
Complaints should be made to an industrial tribunal (see Chapter 9) within 3 months from the date of the matter complained of.

How can the Tribunal help me?
The Tribunal may act as follows:

- Make an order declaring the rights of the parties.

- Award financial compensation.

- Make a recommendation for the discriminator to take action within a specified time.

How do I start my claim?
The first thing to do is to complete Form IT1, *Application to an Industrial Tribunal*. The form itself is fairly straightforward, and a specimen form partly completed is shown overleaf. Then send it to the Central Office of the Industrial Tribunal in London, Glasgow or Belfast, according to where the case arose. Copies of the form are available from offices of the Department of Employment.

Application to an Industrial Tribunal

Please read the notes opposite before filling in this form.

1 Say what type of complaint(s) you want the tribunal to decide *(see note opposite)*

Race Discrimination.

2 Give your name and address etc. in CAPITALS *(see note opposite)*

Mr/Mrs
Miss/Ms

Address

Telephone

Date of birth

3 Please give the name and address of your representative, if you have one.

Name

Address

Telephone

4 Give the name and address of the employer, person or body (the respondent) you are complaining about *(see note opposite)*

Name *Acme Secretarial Services*

Address

Telephone

Give the place where you worked or applied for work, if different from above.

Name

Address

Telephone

5 Please say what job you did for the employer (or what job you applied for). If this does not apply, please say what your connection was with the employer.

Typist.

IT 1 and IT 1(Scot) (Revised July 1987)

Please continue overleaf

6 Please give the number of normal basic hours you worked per week.

Hours [   ] per week

7 Basic wage / salary £ [   ] per [   ]

Average take home pay £ [   ] per [   ]

Other bonuses / benefits £ [   ] per [   ]

8 Please give the dates of your employment *(if applicable)*

Began on [   ]

Ended on [   ]

9 If your complaint is **not** about dismissal, please give the date when the action you are complaining about took place (or the date when you first knew about it).

Date [   ]

10 Give the full details of your complaint *(see note opposite).*

I was employed by Acme Secretarial Services from 1985 until 1991.

On 22nd May 1991, I overheard one of the managers say : " Get the typing done by the wog. "

I claim compensation for race discrimination .

11 Unfair dismissal claimants only (Please tick a box to show what you would want if you win your case).

[ ] Reinstatement: to carry on working in your old job as before

[ ] Re-engagement: to start another job, or a new contract, with your old employer
Orders for reinstatement or re-engagement normally include an award of compensation for loss of earnings.

[✓] Compensation only: to get an award of money
You can change your mind later. The Tribunal will take your preference into account, but will not be bound by it.

Signature: Date:

Printed in the UK for HMSO 12/87 D4 R041092 C2099 TP (192321)

What are exemplary damages?

The term **exemplary damages** means extra damages which are awarded to punish the employer. A recent case concerned Bradford City Council.

Mrs A, a Sikh, was the head of the department of multi-cultural education at a College. She applied for the post of head of department of teaching studies. An industrial tribunal decided that she had been discriminated against in the way in which her application was dealt with. The tribunal awarded exemplary damages against the employer, a local authority.

The authority appealed to the EAT which upheld the appeal on the basis that the actions complained of had been private actions of the council as employer, not as a public local authority.

Mrs A won her appeal to the Court of Appeal. That court said that there was no difference, in discrimination cases, between the public and the private functions of local authorities (*Arora v Bradford City Council, 1990*).

How much compensation could I get?

If discrimination is proved, the tribunal or court would consider what financial loss or expenses the injured party had suffered as a result of the discrimination. This might for example cover:

- loss of pay and other employment benefits, actual and prospective;
- expenses to which the injured party had been put.

Damages for unlawful discrimination are not however limited to the financial loss that can be specifically proved. It is impossible to say what is fair restitution for the injury to feelings, humiliation and insult. The answer must depend on the experience and good sense of the judge or members of the tribunal.

Compensation for a black prisoner at Parkhurst

The question of appropriate compensation arose in a case involving a prisoner at Parkhurst Prison. A black prisoner claimed that he had not been allowed to work in the prison kitchens on grounds of his race. His induction report stated that 'he shows the anti-authoritarian arrogance that seems to be common in most coloured inmates'. The judge found that he had been unlawfully discriminated against on racial grounds. The prisoner was awarded £50 compensation for injury to his feelings.

The Court of Appeal found that the judge had erred, and that the damages would be increased to £500. Awards for injury to feelings should not be minimal, as this would tend to trivialise the public policy to which the 1976 Act gives effect. On the other hand, awards should be restrained just because it is impossible to assess the monetary value of injured feelings (*Alexander v the Home Office*, 1988).

8
Your Rights to
Health and Safety at Work

This chapter deals with the following topics:

- the legal framework for health and safety at work
- specific legislation
- health and safety rights in common law
- social security
- European Community Law

THE LEGAL FRAMEWORK

Your rights to health and safety at work are broadly speaking protected in two ways:

- by specific legislation. The key statutes are the **Factories Act 1961** and the **Health & Safety at Work Act 1974**. There are other statutes as well, as we shall see, and many regulations have been enacted under the authority of these Acts;

- the general common law, and specifically the well-established law of negligence, with its bearing on **safe systems of work**. This covers all aspects of providing a safe working environment and working practices, for instance providing well maintained machinery and equipment. The employer must ensure the safe handling, storing and transportation of articles and substances. The place of work must be maintained to a high degree of safety with sufficient entrances and exits. The employer must provide staff with information, training and supervision to ensure health and safety at work.

Legal definitions

'Practicable and reasonable'
As with many areas of law, the exact meanings of words and terms are

crucially important in the area of Health and Safety at Work. For example, many of the employer's duties are subject to the overriding condition that they must be 'practicable' or 'reasonably practicable'. It is clear that the precise definition of this term can make all the difference between conviction and acquittal for breach of the rules.

'Process'
The word 'process' has also been the subject of much litigation, particularly in relation to the Asbestos Regulations. These state that an employer must provide respiratory equipment where asbestos dust is likely to escape during a 'process'. The courts have held that 'process' means something more than a 'one-off' activity, but need not amount to a long-term factory process.

Importance of other legal definitions
Other terms which have been judicially defined include 'place of work', 'in the course of employment' and 'equipment'. It is important to note that the exact legal meaning of such phrases may not always coincide with their ordinary meaning. It is also important to know that there are established legal definitions of 'office', 'shop' and 'factory'. A 'factory', for example, means something much wider than the normal idea of industrial premises.

SPECIFIC LEGISLATION

Several important Acts of Parliament concerning health and safety at work have been enacted in recent years. They can be summarised as follows:

- The Factories Act 1961
- The Offices, Shops and Railway Premises Act 1963
- The Employers' Liability (Defective Equipment) Act 1969
- The Fire Precautions Act 1971
- The Health & Safety at Work Act 1974
- The Occupiers Liability Act 1984

Of these, the ones of most general importance for employees are the Factories Act and the Health and Safety at Work Act.

Acts of Parliament often empower a government department to issue regulations under an Act, setting out the legal requirements in more detail. Important examples of such statutory regulations are:

- The Construction (Working Places) Regulations 1966
- The Protection of Eyes Regulations 1974
- The Asbestos Regulations
- The Notification of Accidents and Dangerous Occurrences Regulations
- The Control of Substances Hazardous to Health Regulations 1988

Of these, the last has the most far-reaching importance.

We will consider each of these Acts and Regulations in turn.

The Factories Act 1961

This Act forms the basis of modern health and safety law. It sets out detailed rules for health and safety in 'factories', covering such matters as:

- cleanliness
- ventilation
- lighting
- fencing of machinery
- control of dust and fumes
- handling of excessive weights

Detailed rules are also laid down by the Factories Act, and Regulations made under it, in respect of:

- overcrowding
- drainage and sanitation
- floors, passages and stairs
- building operations

Much of this statutory material has been discussed and analysed in very great detail by the courts, so that legal precedents now exist for a whole range of typical situations. To take just one example, in a recent case it was held that a cable attached to a machine for the purpose of supplying power was not an 'obstruction' for the purposes of the Act.

Offices, Shops and Railway Premises Act 1963

This Act provides a basic code of safety law for premises other than factories. It must be remembered that the Factories Act 1961 may still apply, in view of the extended meaning of 'factory'. But the 1963 legislation is to all intents and purposes the same as that of 1961. All the decided cases on parallel provisions of the Act of 1961 also apply to the Offices, Shops and Railway Premises Act.

Employers' Liability (Defective Equipment) Act 1969

This Act makes employers liable for injuries caused by equipment they supply to employees for the purposes of their work, even though the defect was attributable to someone else, such as the manufacturer. The aim of the Act is to safeguard employees from having to sue a manufacturer and prove negligence.

Fire Precautions Act 1971

This sets out the requirements for fire safety in all places of work. All employees must know what to do in case of fire—this may include training in the use of fire extinguishers, locations of fire exits, fire drills—depending on the size and nature of the business.

Fire safety is supervised by the **Fire Authority** who control the issue of **Fire Certificates**. These are required by most businesses but some small businesses may be exempt.

The Health and Safety at Work Act 1974

What are the aims of this important piece of legislation?
- to provide a code of general principles;
- to provide an enforcement procedure;
- to oversee compliance with the Act.

Section 2 of the Act states that it is the duty of every employer to ensure, so far as is **reasonably practicable**, the health, safety and welfare at work of all his employees.

Which firms are covered by the Act?
Almost all employers are affected, including individuals, firms, partnerships, companies, nationalised concerns and government departments. Even self-employed individuals need to be aware of their responsibilities under the statute, for example in relation to the availability of first-aid materials at their place of work (see below).

Workplaces such as factories, offices, shops, workshops, restaurants, schools and colleges are all covered by this rule. It has been estimated that 8 million people are protected by the 1974 Act.

IMPROVEMENT NOTICE

Health and Safety Executive
Health and Safety at Work etc Act 1974, Sections 21, 23 and 24

Serial Number

I

Improvement notice

Name
Address
Trading as*

Inspector's full name   I,

Inspector's official   one of her Majesty's Inspectors of
designation   Being an Inspector appointed by an instrument in writing made
                            pursuant to section 19 of the said Act and entitled to issue this
                            notice

Official address   of

Telephone number

hereby give you notice that I am of the opinion that

Location of premises   at
or place of activity

you, as an employer/a self employed person/a person wholly or
partly in control of the premises/other* are contravening/have
contravened in circumstances that make it likely that the
contravention will continue to be repeated* the following
statutory provisions;

The reasons for my said opinion are:

and I hereby require you to remedy the said contraventions or,
as the case may be, the matters occasioning them by
                            (and I direct that the measures
specified in the Schedule which forms part of this Notice shall
be taken to remedy the said contraventions or matters)*

Signature   Date

An Improvement Notice is also being served on

of

related to the matters contained in this notice

An example of an Improvement Notice.

PROHIBITION NOTICE

Health and Safety Executive
Health and Safety at Work etc Act 1974, Sections 22, 23 and 24

Serial Number

P

Prohibition notice

Name

Address

Trading as*

Inspector's full name

I,

Inspector's official
designation

one of Her Majesty's Inspectors of
Being an Inspector appointed by an instrument in writing made
pursuant to section 19 of the said Act and entitled to issue this
notice

Official address

of

Telephone number

hereby give you notice that I am of the opinion that the following
activities namely:

which are being carried on by you/likely to be carried on by
your/under your control* at

Location of premises
or place of activity

involve, or will involve, a risk of serious personal injury, and that
the matters which give rise/will give rise* to the said risk(s) are:

and that the said matters involve/will involve* contravention of
the following statutory provisions:

because

and I hereby direct that the said activities shall not be carried
out by you or under your control immediately/after*
unless the said contravention(s)* and matters have been
remedied.

I further direct that the measures specified in the schedule
which forms part of this notice shall be taken to remedy the
said contravention(s)* or matters.

Signature

Date

*A Prohibition Notice is also being served on

of

related to the matters contained in this notice

Example of a Prohibition Notice.

What happens if my employer breaks the Act?
Breach of the Act's provisions is a **criminal offence**. Individuals, including directors and company secretaries, can be sentenced to a maximum of two years' imprisonment for a variety of offences under the Act.

How is the Act enforced?
The law is enforced by the Health and Safety Commission, and by the Health and Safety Executive inspectorates. Health and Safety Inspectors have very far-ranging powers. If an inspector finds your firm in breach of the relevant statutory provisions he may issue it with either:

- an **improvement notice** which states that the breach must be remedied within a specified period, or

- a **prohibition notice** demanding that activities, which he has identified as causing serious risk of injury, stop immediately unless remedied.

Appeals against these notices go to the industrial tribunal. The inspector can close down single machines or entire processes and sites if the law has not been complied with. Recently, inspectors have issued improvement notices requiring employers to remove large amounts of asbestos, and to provide a system of training for fork-lift truck drivers.

The Health and Safety Executive has recently mounted a campaign to deal with dangerous building sites. On 2,000 sites out of 8,000 inspected, dangerous processes were forcibly stopped, or the whole operation shut down.

There are Inspectorate addresses throughout the country and one of the head offices will be able to put you in touch with the right one:

Health and Safety Inspectorate
Baynards House
1 Chepstow Place
London W2 4TF
Tel: (071) 229 3456

Health and Safety Inspectorate
Magdalen House
Trinity Road
Merseyside L20 3QZ
Tel: (051) 951 4000

Does anything have to be reported?
Your employer has a legal obligation to report any:

- fatal accidents

- major injury accidents/conditions
- dangerous occurrences
- accidents causing more than three days incapacity for work
- certain work-related diseases
- certain matters dealing with the safe supply of gas

Must the firm keep a record of accidents?
All accidents must be recorded in an **accident book**. This must be kept on the premises and be available for inspection for at least three years after the accident. It should record:

- the date and time of the accident:
- the name of the injured person and details of the injury;
- the place where the accident happened;
- a brief description of the circumstances.

Reportable diseases are those which are work-related. They include certain cases of poisoning, skin diseases, lung diseases, infections and other conditions.

In the case of a reportable disease the employer should record:

- the date of diagnosis;
- the name and occupation of the person affected;
- the name and nature of the disease.

Am I entitled to first aid treatment at work?
Every employer must have at least one **First Aid Box**. It must be clearly identified (ideally green with a white cross on it) and suitable for the purpose. It should keep the contents free from damp and dust. Some employees may need travelling first-aid kits.

The box should contain:

Item	*Number of employees*		
	1-5	6-10	11-50
First-aid guidance card	1	1	1
Individually wrapped sterile adhesive dressings	10	20	40
Sterile eye pads with attachment	1	2	4
Triangular bandages	1	2	4
Safety pins	6	6	12
Sterile unmedicated dressings			
Medium	3	6	8
Large	1	2	4
Extra large	1	2	4

HEALTH & SAFETY POLICY

The Company is concerned for the health, safety and welfare of all its employees, so far as is reasonably practicable, under the terms of the Health and Safety at Work Act. In order to comply with the provisions of the Act, the Company's health and safety policy is as follows:

- To provide and maintain a safe and healthy working environment for all its employees, customers and others legitimately using the Company's premises.
- To ensure that all employees receive adequate information, instruction and training for the evacuation of the Company's premises in the event of fire or other emergency.
- To investigate any accident occurring on the Company's premises, analyse its cause and take any corrective action.
- To provide all employees with the necessary information, instruction, training and supervision to work safely and efficiently.
- To ensure that, as far as is reasonably practicable, any plant, machinery or equipment provided for use is safe in its operation.
- To ensure that adequate first-aid facilities are available within the Company.
- To ensure that all employees are aware of their legal and moral obligations to take reasonable care for the health and safety of themselves and others, by observing all safety regulations and promptly reporting any potential hazards to the Company Safety Officer.

Every Head of Department, and in his absence appointed deputy, has a day-to-day responsibility to ensure safe and healthy working conditions in his own area, and ensuring that employees are familiar with Company policy in respect of safety, fire precautions and first aid. Work routines should be regularly reviewed to ensure that only the safest work practices, use of machines, etc. are followed.

A copy of the 1974 Health and Safety at Work Act can be obtained from the Personnel Department.

Specimen employer's statement of health & safety policy.

More supplies are required if there are over 50 staff.

If there are fewer than 150 staff and they are working in a low hazard business it is only necessary to have an 'Appointed Person' to deal with first aid. If there are serious hazards in your firm, or there are over 150 staff, one or more of the staff must be trained and qualified in first aid. Recognised courses are run by the St. John Ambulance Brigade amongst others. Employees must be informed of the arrangements made for first aid and all first aid treatments must be recorded.

Full details regarding first aid entitlements are available from HMSO. Ask for *The Approved Code of Practice* and *The Guidance Notes* prepared by the Health and Safety Executive.

Must my employer tell me its policy on health and safety?
If your employer employs more than four people working at any one time, it has to issue a **statement** setting out its policy on health and safety. The Health & Safety Executive have never issued a model statement for employers to follow. The circumstances can vary so much from one firm to another. In general the more hazardous the business, the more detailed the statement should be. There is an example of an employer's policy statement opposite.

Do employees have obligations as to health and safety at work?
Yes. It is important to realise that employees also have a duty to take reasonable care for the health and safety of themselves and others who may be affected by their acts and omissions at work. Employees must also co-operate to comply with the statutory requirements laid down.

What are safety representatives?
Some firms have a safety adviser or safety representative. Where there is a recognised union, the union may have a right to appoint safety representatives from the workforce. If two or more such representatives request that a safety committee be formed, the employer has a statutory duty to comply.

A recent case on 'safe system of work'
The following case history illustrates more clearly what is meant by a **safe system of work**.

Ms Daly worked as a clerk in a building society. The office was protected by armoured glass, alarms, a steel plate and a dummy camera. There were two armed robberies. Ms Daly resigned because she was too frightened to carry on working in the office, and claimed constructive dismissal for her employers' failure to provide a safe system of work.

The industrial tribunal upheld her complaint, deciding that the precautions had been inadequate. On appeal the EAT decided that the precautions were those which would have been taken by a reasonable employer, and there had been no constructive dismissal (*Dutton & Clark v Daly*, 1986).

Special regulations

A very large number of Special Regulations have been introduced under the Factories Act 1961 and its predecessors. These deal with particular industries, and some have more general application. The **Construction (Working Places) Regulations** 1966 contain very detailed rules on the safety of scaffolds and ladders. Other regulations of more general significance include the **Protection of Eyes Regulations 1974** and the **Asbestos Regulations**.

The **Notification of Accidents and Dangerous Occurrences Regulations** impose a legal duty upon employers to notify any death, major injury, 'time lost' injury or dangerous occurrence to the enforcing authority.

The Control of Substances Hazardous to Health Regulations 1988

This is the most important Health and Safety legislation since the 1974 Act. It came into effect in October 1989, and aims to control the exposure of employees to hazardous substances whilst at work.

Employers must ensure that suitable and sufficient assessments are made of every hazardous substance used or generated in the workplace. When a risk of exposure has been identified the exposure must be eliminated or, if this is not possible, adequately controlled. Employees who are exposed must receive monitoring and health surveillance.

Employers must instruct, inform and train all employees who may be exposed to hazardous substances at work.

HEALTH AND SAFETY RIGHTS IN COMMON LAW

As we have seen, many of the duties imposed on employers by the Health and Safety legislation can lead to criminal prosecution and penalties. However, they can also give rise to liability under the common law in the civil courts at the same time. In other words, an employee who suffers from wrong treatment at the hands of his employer can sue that employer for damages (financial compensation).

For example, breach of the rules as to fencing dangerous machinery, ventilation and clothing have all led to damages being awarded against employers. In a recent case an employee was awarded a total of £7,000 for the loss of two fingers in an unsafe machine. An independent contractor, for example a window cleaner, may also be entitled to compensation through civil proceedings where the employer has failed to provide a 'safe system of work'.

Employers' legal duty of care

In addition to the legal duties set out in statutes and regulations, employers are subject to an additional set of duties imposed by common law. These duties co-exist with the statutory obligations. Employees often make claims alleging breach of statutory duty and, in the alternative, breach of a common law duty. The most frequent common law duty allegedly broken is the general obligation to take care for the safety of employees. This is often described as **negligence** and is subject to all the general rules of common law negligence rather than the statutory provisions. It is the employer's duty to reduce risks to the employee as fast as is 'reasonably practicable'.

If a job cannot be made absolutely safe, the employer must do all he can to make it as safe as can reasonably be expected in the circumstances. This may mean going further than currently accepted trade practices. The employer's duty is to take reasonable steps to prevent injury to employees or others who, with reasonable foresight, are likely to be injured by the employer's activities. This is an all-embracing duty and extends to the whole of every factory, office and workplace. It is the duty of every employer:

1. to avoid injuring an employee by a positive act of negligence;

2. to prevent injury to the employee by a failure to act.

Employer's duty to warn of risks

It is also important to note that there is a growing body of law on the employer's duty to positively warn employees about dangers to health which might be involved with a job. In general, it is the positive duty of employers to ensure that employees are instructed in the standards required by the legislation.

Obligations of employees

It is important to note that employees, too, have a general **duty of care** both to themselves and towards their fellow employees. An employee who suffers injury at work for example could not hold his employer liable for negligence if the injury arose solely from the employee's own obvious carelessness.

The employer may have issued disciplinary rules and procedures for the proper application of health and safety law. An employee who breaks those rules might be liable to dismissal.

How an employee's claim might fail

If breach of statutory duty, or negligence, is established, there are five possible defences which an employer may raise.

1. Lack of causation—although there has been a breach of statutory duty, the injury was not caused by the breach.

2. The claimant's own fault contributed to his injury (contributory negligence). In one recent case, an employee's damages were reduced by 40% because of his failure to wear safety goggles provided for his use.

3. The breach of duty was brought about entirely by the fault of the employee.

4. The employee completely voluntarily and knowingly exposed himself to risk (the Latin maxim *Volenti non fit injuria*).

5. Limitation of time. Too many years had elapsed before the original claim was made.

Amount of compensation

The amount of damages which the courts are likely to award for injuries suffered at work are of great importance. English courts have given judgment in a very large number of cases dealing with industrial and personal injuries, and it is possible for an experienced legal adviser to predict with some accuracy the potential value of an accident.

Employer's Liability Insurance
An employer has a **statutory duty** to take out Employer's Liability

Insurance. This is to cover personal injuries or diseases suffered by employees during the course of, or arising because of, their employment.

This insurance must be taken out with an **authorised insurer** and the certificate issued must be **displayed** at the place of work, where all employees can see it.

SOCIAL SECURITY

None of the above material on health and safety at work should be considered in isolation from the social security system. Both employers and employees need to know the details of sick pay schemes and government payments for industrial injuries and diseases. These schemes operate in conjunction with the common law rights and duties described above.

EUROPEAN COMMUNITY LAW

As the United Kingdom becomes more involved with the detailed rules of the EC in relation to trade and industry, the law and practice of health and safety at work is likely to reflect an increasingly European influence. Some of the EEC directives in this area are extremely complex, and the English courts have already had to grapple with the very difficult problem of applying the rules on goods vehicle drivers' hours. Employers will certainly need to be more aware of EEC regulations as 1992 approaches.

9
Going to an Industrial Tribunal

This chapter deals with the following matters:

- constitution and powers of industrial tribunals
- applying to an industrial tribunal
- hearings
- decisions
- appeals
- Advisory, Conciliation and Arbitration Service (ACAS)

CONSTITUTION

The Tribunal normally consists of a legally-qualified chairman sitting with two industrial members. These are appointed from lists provided by the CBI and the TUC.

POWERS (JURISDICTION)

Aspects of employment law covered by Industrial Tribunals include:

- unfair dismissal

- redundancy payment disputes

- race and sex discrimination

- appeals against prohibition and improvement notices under the Health and Safety at Work Act 1974.

APPLYING TO AN INDUSTRIAL TRIBUNAL

The application procedure is quite straightforward, and the whole process is very much simpler, more informal and cheaper than the alternative of going to court.

Form IT1

The first step is to obtain and complete *Form IT1*, Application to an Industrial Tribunal. A specimen of this is shown on pages 114-16. Copies of the form can be obtained from several places including:

- trade unions
- Jobcentres
- Unemployment Benefit Offices
- other offices of the employment service

How to complete the form

It is not necessary to go into great detail at this stage. A brief statement of the facts upon which your claim is based will be enough. The employer can if he wishes ask for more details if necessary.

Where to send the form

The form must be sent to the Central Office of the Industrial Tribunals (see list of useful addresses at end of book). This office will then forward it to the employer, who may set out his own case in *Form IT3*. The case will normally be heard within 6 to 8 weeks.

Time limits for claims

It must be sent within the time limit, normally three months. The Tribunal has the power to extend this limit but it is normally better to keep to time.

The case of the late claimant

Miss R was dismissed on June 2, 1989. The last day for presenting a complaint of unfair dismissal to an industrial tribunal was September 1. She was advised by a Citizens Advice Bureau worker that the complaint had to be received by September 2. The CAB worker was told by an employee of an industrial tribunal that the complaint need not be presented until September 4. The complaint was in fact presented on September 2. The tribunal decided that it could hear the complaint because Miss R was entitled to rely on the advice of the tribunal employee. The employer appealed to the EAT. It was held that failure by an adviser such as a solicitor or a CAB worker to give correct advice prevented employees as a general rule from claiming that it was not reasonable to apply within the three month period. But it was different where the wrong advice was given by an industrial tribunal employee (*Jean Sorelle Ltd v Ryback*, 1990).

Application to an Industrial Tribunal

Filling in the form

Help: Your Trade Union or local Citizens' Advice Bureau may be able to help you fill in the form if you have any problems, but make sure your form arrives within the TIME LIMIT.

Questions to answer: Try to complete all the boxes that apply in your case. You MUST answer the questions in boxes 1, 2, 4, 8 and 10.

Be clear: This form has to be photocopied, so please use black ink, or type your answers, and use CAPITAL LETTERS for names and addresses.

Box 1
Put here the type of complaint you want the Tribunal to decide (for example, unfair dismissal, redundancy payment, equal pay, etc.). A full list of types of complaint is given in the leaflet ITL1. If there is more than one complaint you want the Tribunal to decide, please say so. Give the details of your complaints in Box 10.

Box 2
Give your name and address and date of birth, and if possible a telephone number where the Tribunal or ACAS can contact you during the day about your application.

Box 4
Put here the name and address of the employer, person or body (the "respondent") you wish to complain about. In the second box, give also the place where you worked or applied for work, if different from that of the respondent you have named. (For example, complete both boxes if you have named a liquidator, the Secretary of State for Employment, or your employer's Head Office as the respondent).

Box 10
Give full details of your complaint. If there is not enough room on the form, continue on a separate sheet, and attach it to the form. Do NOT send any other documents or evidence in support of your complaint at this stage. Your answer may be used in an initial assessment of your case, so make it as complete and accurate as you can. (See **Help** above).

When you have finished:

- **Sign and date the form**
- **Keep these Guidance Notes and a copy of your answers**
- **Send the form to:**

ENGLAND AND WALES:

**The Secretary of the Tribunals,
Central Office of the Industrial
  Tribunals
93 Ebury Bridge Road
London SW1W 8RE
Tel: 01-730 9161**

SCOTLAND:

**The Secretary of the Tribunals
Central Office of Industrial
  Tribunals (Scotland)
St Andrew House,
141 West Nile Street
Glasgow G1 2RU
Tel: 041-331 1601**

Application to an Industrial Tribunal

Please read the notes opposite before filling in this form.

1 Say what type of complaint(s) you want the tribunal to decide *(see note opposite)*

Unfair Dismissal.

2 Give your name and address etc. in CAPITALS *(see note opposite)*

Mr/Mrs
Miss/Ms

Address

Telephone

Date of birth

3 Please give the name and address of your representative, if you have one.

Name

Address

Telephone

4 Give the name and address of the employer, person or body (the respondent) you are complaining about *(see note opposite)*

Name *Acme Secretarial Services*

Address

Telephone

Give the place where you worked or applied for work, if different from above.

Name

Address

Telephone

5 Please say what job you did for the employer (or what job you applied for). If this does not apply, please say what your connection was with the employer.

Filing Clerk.

IT 1 and IT 1(Scot) (Revised July 1987)

Please continue overleaf

6 Please give the number of normal basic hours you worked per week.

Hours [   ] per week

7 Basic wage / salary £ [   ] per [   ]

Average take home pay £ [   ] per [   ]

Other bonuses / benefits £ [   ] per [   ]

8 Please give the dates of your employment *(if applicable)*

Began on [   ]

Ended on [   ]

9 If your complaint is **not** about dismissal, please give the date when the action you are complaining about took place (or the date when you first knew about it).

Date [   ]

10 Give the full details of your complaint *(see note opposite)*

I worked for Acme Secretarial Services from 1986 until 1990. In December 1990 I was dismissed as being surplus to requirements.

I do not believe that this was true.

11 Unfair dismissal claimants only (Please tick a box to show what you would want if you win your case).

[✓] Reinstatement: to carry on working in your old job as before

[ ] Re-engagement: to start another job, or a new contract, with your old employer
Orders for reinstatement or re-engagement normally include an award of compensation for loss of earnings.

[ ] Compensation only: to get an award of money
You can change your mind later. The Tribunal will take your preference into account, but will not be bound by it.

Signature: Date:

Printed in the UK for HMSO 12/87 Dd 8041097 C 2000 1P (192321)

HEARINGS

The Tribunal does not operate in the same way as a court of law. Proceedings are meant to be:

- quick
- cheap
- informal

Lawyers do not wear robes.

Some questions and answers

Do I have to be represented by a solicitor?
No. You don't have to be represented at all. You may if you wish be represented by a barrister, solicitor, trade union representative, or simply a friend. Parties appearing without legal representation are normally assisted by the Tribunal.

Can I get legal aid?
No. Legal Aid is not available for industrial tribunal cases.

Will I have to pay costs?
The Tribunal may instruct either side in the dispute to pay costs, where that person has behaved frivolously, vexatiously or unreasonably.

What is the best way to present my case?

- Have all the facts of your case ready to hand—names, dates, places, any notes you made at the time.

- Do not attempt a 'Perry Mason'.

- Let the Chairman run his own Tribunal.

- Allow every witness a fair chance to state his or her case.

- Remember that all the witnesses must give evidence on oath.

- Remain calm and courteous and businesslike throughout.

THE INDUSTRIAL TRIBUNALS

NOTICE OF HEARING

Case No. . . . .

NOTICE IS HEREBY GIVEN THAT THE application of
has been listed for hearing by an Industrial Tribunal at:-

on   day,   19   at   am/pm

1.   Attendance should be at the above time and place. The parties (other than
a respondent who has not entered an appearance) are entitled to appear at the
hearing and to state their case in person or be represented by anyone they wish. A
party can choose not to appear and can rely on written representations (which if
additional to any already submitted must be sent to the Tribunal and copied to the
other party not less than 7 days before the hearing). However, experience shows
that it is normally advisable for a party and any witnesses to attend in person even
if they have made statements or representations in writing.

2.   It is very important that each party should bring to the hearing any
documents that may be relevant, eg a letter of appointment, contract of
employment, Working Rule Agreement, pay slips, income tax forms, evidence of
unemployment and other social security benefit, wages book, details of benefits
and contributions under any pension or superannuation scheme, etc.

3.   If the complaint is one of unfair dismissal or refusal of permission for a
woman employee to return to work after a pregnancy the tribunal may wish to
consider whether to make an order for reinstatement or re-engagement. In these
cases the respondent should be prepared to give evidence at the hearing as to the
availability of the job from which the applicant was dismissed, or held before
absence due to pregnancy, or of comparable or suitable employment and
generally as to the practicability of reinstatement or re-engagement of the
applicant to the respondent.

4.   If for any reason a party (other than a respondent who has not entered an
appearance) does not propose to appear at the hearing, either personally or by a
representative, he should inform me immediately, in writing, giving the reason and
the case number. He should also state whether he wishes the hearing to proceed
in his absence, relying on any written representations he may have made. If an
applicant fails to appear at the hearing the tribunal may dismiss or dispose of the
application in his absence.

5.   The hearing of this case will take place at the time stated above or as soon
thereafter as the tribunal can hear it.

To the Applicant(s) (Ref   )   Signed . . . .
                                                  for Assistant Secretary of the Tribunals

                                                  Date   . . . .

and the Respondent(s) (Ref   )   NOTE Representatives who receive
                                                  this notice must inform the party they
                                                  represent of the date, time and place
                                                  of the hearing. The party will not be
                                                  notified direct.

and the Secretary of State for Employment
and the Conciliation Officer, Advisory Conciliation and Arbitration Service

HOW DECISIONS ARE MADE

Discretionary powers of tribunals

As we saw earlier, the law gives wide discretionary power to industrial
tribunals hearing cases of wrongful or unfair dismissal. Among the
facts they may take into account in particular cases are these:

- How long was the employee employed? Less than two years—no
  unfair dismissal except in matters of trade union activities, race
  or sex discrimination.

- Reason for dismissal—was it reasonable? Did the employee
  contribute to the problem?

- Were disciplinary procedures complied with?

- Were any relevant Codes of Practice observed?

- Was a full investigation carried out before dismissal?

- Could written reasons for the dismissal, enough to satisfy an
  industrial tribunal, be supplied?

- Was or will there be a payment in lieu of notice?

- Has there been a reasonable cooling-off period?

Similar facts—opposite conclusions

Tribunals may adopt rather different approaches to quite similar
problems, as the following contrasting cases illustrate.

No instant dismissal for 'clocking'...
An employee clocked in three others before the return to work after
the lunch-break. The employer had posted notices stating that
'clocking' was regarded as a serious offence and would render
offenders liable to dismissal.

Both the Industrial Tribunal and, on appeal, the Employment
Appeal Tribunal, found that the dismissal was unfair, essentially
because the notices were ambiguous and did not necessarily mean
'instant dismissal' (*Meridian Ltd v Gomersall*, 1977).

THE INDUSTRIAL TRIBUNALS
BETWEEN

Applicant   Respondent

Mr X   AND   Acme
                                             Secretarial
                                             Services

DECISION OF THE INDUSTRIAL TRIBUNAL

HELD AT BRISTOL   ON November 30, 1990

DECISION

The majority decision of the Tribunal is that the Applicant was
unfairly dismissed and we award him as compensation the sum of
£500.

REASONS

_____
_____
_____
_____
_____
_____
_____
_____
_____
_____
_____
_____

Specimen decision of an Industrial Tribunal.

...Instant dismissal for 'clocking'
On the other hand, on very similar facts, the tribunal reached the opposite conclusion in the case of *Stewart* (1978). Their reasoning was based on the fact that 'clocking' was a serious offence of dishonesty justifying instant dismissal. In general, tribunals have tended to follow this approach and to treat dishonesty or violence as instantly dismissable even where fair dismissal procedures have not been strictly complied with.

Don't tribunals have to follow precedents?

The principle of precedent underlies most of English law.

- This means that a court or tribunal is obliged to follow **legal rules** laid down in reported cases heard by courts or tribunals at a higher level.

It is important to note that this relates only to **legal** matters, whereas the vast majority of cases dealt with tribunals are concerned with **fact**, decided on the evidence as to which party is telling the truth.

What if the tribunal itself is biased?

The members of a tribunal are under as great a duty as anyone for example to observe the law regarding sex and racial discrimination. This question arose in 1990 in a case involving a woman police sergeant, and it is interesting to see how it was dealt with, both at the original tribunal and on appeal.

Request to bring a breast-fed child into the tribunal
Mrs Kennedy, a police sergeant, made a discrimination complaint to an industrial tribunal. At the time of the tribunal hearing she was breast feeding her four-week old child. The hearing was interrupted a number of times for the child to be fed. Mrs Kennedy asked if the child could be present in the tribunal room. The chairman stated that she would not have babies, dogs or children in the tribunal and that Mrs Kennedy's counsel could arrange for one of her minions to look after it. Mrs Kennedy applied for the tribunal to disqualify itself on the grounds of bias. The tribunal refused and Mrs Kennedy appealed to the Employment Appeal Tribunal.

The EAT stated that the moderate and temperate use of language was of vital importance. But the behaviour of the tribunal had not amounted to bias (*Kennedy v Commissioner of Police of the Metropolis*, 1990).

How soon is a tribunal decision given?

The decision of the Tribunal may be given immediately or may be **reserved** for a few weeks.

APPEALS

An appeal may be made to the **Employment Appeal Tribunal** (EAT) on a point of law, within six weeks of the decision. The EAT consists of a High Court judge and two unqualified members. Further appeals are possible, with permission, to the Court of Appeal and to the House of Lords. In certain cases there is also a right of appeal to the European Court of Justice.

ACAS (THE ADVISORY CONCILIATION AND ARBITRATION SERVICE)

This is an independent body which operates to promote improved industrial relations and collective bargaining. It may hold its own inquiries, but its normal method of working is to resolve industrial disputes where the parties consistently fail to reach agreement. ACAS conciliation officers assist in the settlement of disputes outside the industrial tribunal. There is no obligation to consult ACAS, but the parties may well find that it is in their interests to do so.

ACAS also prepares voluntary codes of practice which set out suggested rules in areas such as discipline and trade union activities.

List of Statutes

ACCESS TO MEDICAL REPORTS ACT 1988
Gives employees the right of access to any medical report relating to them, supplied by their doctor for employment purposes.

ATTACHMENT OF EARNINGS ACT 1971
The courts may order an employer to make deductions from an employee's pay, and forward them to court, in respect of defaults on a court order to pay a fine, debt or maintenance.

COMPANIES ACTS
Set out in great detail the law governing companies, including the powers and duties of directors.

CONTROL OF SUBSTANCES HAZARDOUS TO HEALTH REGULATIONS 1988
Control the exposure of employees to hazardous substances while at work. Impose detailed responsibilities upon employers to reduce the risk of exposure to hazardous substances.

DATA PROTECTION ACT 1984
Gives employees the right to examine computer records containing information about them.

DISABLED PERSONS (EMPLOYMENT) ACTS 1944, 1958
Impose quotas of disabled people which must be employed by employers above a certain size.

EMPLOYERS' LIABILITY (DEFECTIVE EQUIPMENT) ACT 1969
Makes employers liable for injuries caused by defective equipment even where the defect was the fault of the manufacturer.

EMPLOYMENT ACT 1980
Deals with secret ballots; unreasonable expulsion from trade unions; picketing and secondary action.

EMPLOYMENT ACT 1989
Contains provisions against discrimination in employment and training; removes restrictions on the hours of work of young people; limits paid time off for union duties; empowers tribunals to require a deposit for poorly based claims; and miscellaneous other matters.

EMPLOYMENT PROTECTION ACT 1975
Introduced a wide range of material dealing with employment rights.

EMPLOYMENT PROTECTION (CONSOLIDATION) ACT 1978
Brought together in one statute a very wide range of rules dealing with employment matters.

EQUAL PAY ACT 1970
Introduced the principle that men and women are, generally, entitled to equal pay for similar work.

FACTORIES ACT 1961
This Act, and a large number of Regulations made under it, deals with safety in industrial working places.

HEALTH AND SAFETY AT WORK ACT 1974
Provides a Code of general principles and an enforcement mechanism for health and safety matters.

OFFICES, SHOPS AND RAILWAY PREMISES ACT 1963
Applies the Factories Act 1961 to a wide range of other premises.

RACE RELATIONS ACT 1976
Sets out the law governing race discrimination.

REHABILITATION OF OFFENDERS ACT 1974
Allows persons convicted of relatively minor offences, after a period of non-offending, to have their convictions treated as 'spent'. A job applicant is not obliged to admit to a spent conviction, and may not be dismissed or discriminated against on the grounds of that conviction.

SEX DISCRIMINATION ACT 1975
Sets out the law governing sex discrimination.

TRADE UNION ACT 1984
Deals with trade union elections and sets out new rules for industrial
action.

WAGES ACT 1986
Deals with deductions from wages.

Glossary

This glossary of technical legal terms is designed for use by non-lawyers. It covers, in particular, words with legal meanings which may differ from their everyday meanings. This glossary is intended to meet the demands of those concerned with employment rights, for explanations of lawyers' jargon. Some of the explanations below deal only with the meanings of words and phrases in the context of rights at work.

Act. A law passed by the House of Commons and the House of Lords, and signed by the Queen.

Action. Proceedings in a court.

Appellant. A person who makes an appeal. In the area of employment rights, this will normally be to the Employment Appeal Tribunal (EAT) from the Industrial Tribunal, or to the Court of Appeal from the EAT.

Arbitration. The settling of a dispute by an arbitrator, and not by the courts or tribunals.

Civil (Action, Court, Law). That part of English law which deals with private rights as opposed to allegations of crime.

Code. A body of rules for practical guidance, for example the Highway Code, or a Disciplinary Code. These Rules do not have the force of law, but may be used as evidence in court cases.

Collective Agreement. An agreement resulting from bargaining over terms and conditions between trade unions and employers.

Common Law. Traditional unwritten law, contained in judicial decisions.

Compensation. Financial payment for injuries or loss suffered because of an unlawful act.

Conciliation. The settlement of a dispute outside the courts by reference to a conciliator, eg ACAS.

Constructive Dismissal. Indirect dismissal caused by the unreasonable actions of an employer, virtually forcing an employee to resign.

Contract. An agreement intended to create legal obligations.

Contributory Negligence. Carelessness by an injured person which may reduce the amount of compensation payable.

Court of Appeal. The Court which has power to hear appeals on points of law from the EAT.

Criminal. Acts, offences against the State, subject to punishment.

Damages. Money compensation for injury and/or loss.

Defendant. A person against whom an action is brought.

Dismissal. The termination of an employer's contract of employment by the employer. See also **Constructive Dismissal, Summary Dismissal, Unfair Dismissal, Wrongful Dismissal.**

Employee. A person who works under a contract of employment.

Employment Appeal Tribunal (EAT). A body which hears appeals on points of law from Industrial Tribunals.

Fraud. A false statement made dishonestly, intentionally or recklessly.

Guarantee Payment. Payments which employers must make to employees who have been laid off.

Held. Decided.

Industrial Tribunal. A body which deals with complaints in relation to rights at work.

Injunction. A court order requiring a person to do or refrain from doing a particular thing.

Insolvency. Inability to pay debts because of lack of assets.

Legislation. Acts of Parliament.

Liability. The obligation to pay damages.

Negligence. Failure to take reasonable care, resulting in injury to loss to another person.

Plaintiff. A person who brings an action.

Precedent. A judicial decision, creating a rule of law, which applies to later cases involving similar facts.

Procedure. The formal method of carrying on legal proceedings.

Redundancy. Dismissal of an employee where his job has ceased to exist.

Statute. See **Act**.

Summary Dismissal. Instant termination of a contract of employment, without notice.

Tort. Conduct giving rise to a civil action, eg **Negligence, Wrongful Dismissal**. The normal redress is damages or an injunction.

Trade Dispute. A dispute between workers and employers relating for example to terms and conditions of employment.

Trade Union. An organisation of workers with the main purpose of regulating relations between workers and employers.

Unfair Dismissal. A termination of the contract of employment which the law considers unfair, eg for carrying out trade union duties.

Vicarious Liability. The liability of an employer for the conduct of an employee.

Void. Having no legal effect.

Wrongful Dismissal. Unjustified dismissal in breach of the contract of employment.

Further Reading

General publications on employment law

Civil Liberty: The NCCL Guide, Hurwitt & Thornton (Penguin Books, 1989).

Employment Law Manual (Sweet & Maxwell. Looseleaf).

Encyclopedia of Labour Relations Law (Sweet & Maxwell. Looseleaf).

Health & Safety Case Law, Spicer (Croner. Looseleaf).

The Lawbook, Allianz Legal Protection (Jordans, 1987).

Rights at Work, McMullen (Pluto Press, 1984).

Secretarial Adminstration (Jordans. Looseleaf).

Sex Discrimination Law, Pannick (Oxford University Press, 1986).

Textbook on Labour Law, Bowers and Honeyball (Blackstone Press, 1990).

Women and Employment, McLoughlin (WI Books, 1989).

The Worker and the Law, Wedderburn (Penguin Books, 1989).

Free ACAS booklets

Employing People: The ACAS Handbook for Small Firms.

Discipline at Work: The ACAS Advisory Handbook.

Advisory Booklets Series:

    No. 1. – Job Evaluation.

    No. 2. – Introduction to Payment Systems.

    No. 3. – Personnel Records.

    No. 4. – Labour Turnover.

    No. 5. – Absence.

    No. 6. – Recruitment and Selection.

    No. 7. – Induction of New Employees.

    No. 8. – Workplace Communications.

    No. 9. – The Company Handbook.

    No. 10. – Employment Policies.

    No. 11. – Employee appraisal.

    No. 12. – Redundancy handling.

No. 13. – Hours of work.
No. 14. – Appraisal related pay.
No. 15 – Health and Employment.
This is ACAS
Using ACAS in Industrial Disputes
The ACAS Role in Conciliation
Advice and Help
Individual Employment Rights (leaflet)
Individual Employment Rights (booklet)

Free booklets from the Department of Employment

The following are published in the Employment Legislation Series:
Written statement of main terms and conditions of employment
    (PL700)
Employee's rights on insolvency of employer (PL718)
Employment rights for the expectant mother (PL710)
Suspension on medical grounds under health and safety regulations
    (PL705)
Facing redundancy? Time off for job hunting or to arrange training
    (PL703)
Itemized pay statements (PL704)
Guarantee payments (PL724)
Employment rights on the transfer of an undertaking (PL699)
Rules governing continuous employment and a week's pay (PL711)
Time off for public duties (PL702)
Unfairly dismissed? (PL712)
Rights to notice and reasons for dismissal (PL707)
Redundancy payments (PL808)
Redundancy consultation and notification (PL833)
Fair and unfair dismissal: a guide for employers (PL714)
Limits on payments (PL827)
Individual rights of employees: a guide for employers (PL716)
Industrial Tribunal procedure (ITL1)

Union matters

Union secret ballots (PL701)
Trade union executive elections (PL86)
Trade union political funds (PL868)
Trade union funds and accounting records (PL867)
Union membership and non-membership rights (PL871)

Statutory code of practice on closed shop agreements and arrangements
Unjustifiable discipline by a trade union (PL865)
Industrial action and the law: a guide for employees and trade union members (PL869)
Guide to the Trade Union Act 1984 (PL752)
The Employment Act 1988: A guide to its industrial relations and trade union provisions (PL854)
Statutory code of practice on picketing

Commission for Racial Equality

A large number of free and low-priced publications are available from the Commission for Racial Equality. The following is just a selection. For a full list ask for the CRE Publications Mail Order List.

Racial Discrimination: A Guide to the Race Relations Act 1976 (Home Office/COI).
Racial Equality Councils in Britain: a List (1990).
Your Rights to Equal Treatment under the Race Relations Act 1976.
Code of Practice for the Elimination of Racial Discrimination in Education (1989).
Ethnic Minority School Teachers: A Survey in eight local education authorities (1988).
A Guide to the Race Relations Act: Employment.
Code of Practice: for the elimination of racial discrimination and the promotion of equality of opportunity in employment (1983).
Ethnic Minorities and the Graduate Employment Market (1990).
Indirect Discrimination in Employment: A Practical Guide (1989).

The CRE has also published a large number of Formal Investigation Reports (mostly free) into actual cases of alleged racial discrimination.

Useful Addresses

Advisory, Conciliation and Arbitration Service (ACAS), Clifton House, 83 Euston Road, London NW1 2RB. Tel: (071) 388 5100/3041. The main regional offices are as follows:

Northern Region: Westgate House, Westgate Road, Newcastle-upon-Tyne NE1 1TJ. Tel: (091) 261 2191.

Midlands Region: Alpha Tower, Suffolk Street, Queensway, Birmingham B1 1TZ. Tel: (021) 631 3434.

Nottingham Sub-office: 66 Houndsgate, Nottingham NG1 6BA. Tel: (0602) 415450.

North West Region: Boulton House, 17-21 Chorlton Street, Manchester M1 3HY. Tel: (061) 228 3222.

Merseyside Sub-office: Cressington House, 249 St Mary's Road, Garston, Liverpool L19 0NF. Tel: (051) 427 8881.

Scotland: Franborough House, 123-157 Bothwell Street, Glasgow G2 7JR. Tel: (041) 204 2677.

Wales: Phase 1, Ty Glas Road, Llanishen, Cardiff CF4 5PH. Tel: (0222) 762636.

Yorkshire and Humberside Region: Commerce House, St Alban's Place, Leeds LS2 8HH. Tel: (0532) 431371.

South East Region: Westminster House, Fleet Road, Fleet, Hants GU13 8PD. Tel: (0252) 811868.

South-West Region: Regent House, 27A Regent Street, Clifton, Bristol BS8 4HR. Tel: (0272) 744066.

Association of British Insurers, Aldermary House, 10-15 Queen Street, London EC4N 1TT. Tel: (071) 248 4477.

Central Arbitration Committee, 39 Grosvenor Place, London SW1X 7BD. Tel: (071) 210 3738.

Central Office of Industrial Tribunals (COIT) (England and Wales), 93 Ebury Bridge Road, London SW1W 8RT. Tel: (071) 730 9161.

Certification Officer, 27 Wilton Street, London SW1X 7AZ. Tel: (071) 210 3734.

Citizens Advice Bureaux. Branches nationwide.

Commission for Racial Equality, Elliot House, 10-12 Allington Street, London SW1E 5EH. Tel: (071) 828 7022.

Companies House, 55-71 City Road, London EC1Y 1BB. Tel: (071) 253 9393.

Data Protection Registrar, Springfield House, Water Lane, Wilmslow, Cheshire SK9 5AX. Tel: (0625) 535777.

Department of Employment/Employment Service, Caxton House, Tothill Street, London SW1H 9NF. Tel: (071) 231 4033.

DOE Redundancy Payments Offices

Chesser House West (5th Floor), 502 Gorgie Road, Edinburgh EH11 3YH. Tel: (031) 443 8731. *Areas covered*: Scotland, Cleveland, Cumbria, Durham, Northumberland, Tyne and Wear.

Aytoun Street, Manchester M60 2HS. Tel: (061) 236 4433. *Areas covered*: Cheshire, Greater Manchester, Humberside, Lancashire, Merseyside, Yorkshire.

2 Duchess Place, Hagley Road, Birmingham B16 8NS. Tel: (021) 456 1144. *Areas covered*: Avon, Bedfordshire, Buckinghamshire, Cambridgeshire, Cornwall, Derbyshire, Devon, Dorset, Gloucestershire, Hereford and Worcester, Leicestershire, Lincolnshire, Norfolk, Northamptonshire, Nottinghamshire, Oxfordshire, Shropshire, Somerset, Staffordshire, Suffolk, Warwickshire, West Midlands, Wiltshire, Wales.

Arena House, North End Road, Wembley HA9 0NF. Tel: (081) 900 1966. *Area covered*: all other counties plus London.

Department of Social Security (for leaflets), Market Towers, 1 Nine Elms Lane, London SW8 5NQ. Tel: (071) 720 2188.

Employment Appeals Tribunal, 4 St James' Square, London SW1. Tel: (071) 210 3000.

Equal Opportunities Commission, Overseas House, Quay Street, Manchester M3 3HN. Tel: (061) 833 9244.

Health & Safety Commission, 1 Baynard House, 1 Chepstow Place, London W2 4TF. Tel: (071 221 8070).

Her Majesty's Stationery Office (HMSO), 49 High Holborn, London WC1V 6HB. Tel: (071) 622 3316. Publisher of a vast array of government and official publications.

Institute of Directors, 116 Pall Mall, London SW1. Tel: (071) 839 1233.

Law Society, 113 Chancery Lane, London WC2. Tel: (071) 242 1222. The solicitors' professional body.

Legal Aid, 29-37 Red Lion Street, London WC1R 4PP. Tel: (071) 405 6991.

National Council for Civil Liberties (NCCL), 21 Tabard Street, London SE1 4LA. Tel: (071) 403 3888.

Occupation Pensions Board, Apex Tower, High Street, New Malden, Surrey KT3 4DN. Tel: (081) 942 8949.

Trades Union Council (TUC), Congress House, Great Russell Street, London WC1B 3LS. Tel: (071) 636 4030.

Workers Educational Association (WEA), 32 Tavistock Square, London WC1. Tel: (071) 388 7261.

Index

How to Know Your Rights: Students
Shirley Meredeen BA

Students today often find themselves faced with a bewildering range of problems, involving for example their college, local authorities, landlords, banks, doctors, employers, shopkeepers, and government departments such as the DSS. This new student-friendly paperback guide meets an enormous need for basic information on the academic, financial and social rights of all students in secondary, further or higher education. In plain English it explains students' rights in everything from demos to drug-busts, grants and allowances, sexual relationships, discrimination, to choice of study, accommodation, appeals and a host of other important matters. The book is complete with practical checklists and key reference information. Shirley Meredeen has long experience of counselling and advising students of all backgrounds. Formerly Accommodation Officer at the Polytechnic of North London, then Student Services Officer at the City & East London College, she is now a freelance consultant, trainer and counsellor.

208pp illustrated paperback. 1 85703 001 X

How to Know Your Rights: Teachers
Neil Adams

In the wake of the recent Education Reform Acts, this new book meets an urgent need for a clear statement as to where teachers stand from a professional and legal point of view. In plain English it clarifies such vital matters as recruitment procedures, the legal basis of terms and conditions of service, grievance and disciplinary procedures, dismissal of teachers, union membership, sexual, racial and other discrimination, absences from duty, negligence, the concept of in loco parentis, and numerous other sensitive and timely matters. Complete with checklists, sample documents and essential reference information. Neil Adams is a specialist in the field of Education Law. The author of the earlier text *Law and Teachers Today*, he lectures regularly on the subject at several Universities, Management Centres, Colleges and Teachers Centres. A secondary Head of 26 years' standing, he is also an Open University Tutor in Education Management.

144pp illustrated paperback. 1 85703 002 8

How to Claim State Benefits
Martin Rathfelder *Second edition*

Many claimants are understandably put off by the jungle of rules, regulations and paperwork. This is the first popular paperback to be published which explains in clear and simple language exactly what are every citizen's rights and entitlements under the law. Laid out in a quick reference A to Z format it covers a vast range of information in concise form. As featured on 'What Would You Do' (Tyne-Tees Television) 'Money Box (BBC Radio 2) 'This is Your Right' (Granada Television). Martin Rathfelder is Adviser at the Welfare Rights Unit,

Manchester. He has also been Treasurer of the Greater Manchester Campaign Against Social Security Cuts and Welfare Rights Officer for the Citizens Advice Bureau.

224pp illustrated paperback 0 7464 0531 1 Second edition.

How to Survive at College
David Acres

This informed and very readable guide makes riveting reading for everyone who wants to know what they should really expect as to studies and teaching, revision and exams, money, accommodation, social life, personal relationships, vacations, and much besides. 'A useful guide to the numerous problems that may confront the new student... Mr Acres' experience as a student counsellor has given him a very good idea of how students approach their new lifestyle and the range of problems they face... Humorous and informative.' *Times Higher Educational Supplement.* David Acres is a Senior Lecturer and Counsellor at the Student Services Centre, Polytechnic Southwest.

128pp illustrated paperback. 0 7463 0507 9.

How to Run a Local Campaign
Polly Bird

As people battle against vested interests for a better life, this book explains in a clear easy-to-read format the right approach to starting and winning a public campaign. Polly Bird, herself an experienced local campaigner, provides tips, advice and checklists from first steps and publicity through to funds, self-help options, and what to do on completion of a project. Including valuable campaigning address lists, this book is a must for everyone with a cause to fight. 'An excellent beginner's guide to successful campaigning.' *Green Magazine.* 'Contains everything the local activist needs to know.' *Dulwich Labour Party Newsletter.* 'Can help would-be campaign organisers to avoid many of the pitfalls and heartaches ahead.' *Conservative Newsline.* 'Polly Bird is someone that those in authority would be wise not to upset. Her book is a must for all who want to cause authority a headache...' *The Chemical Engineer.*

144pp illustrated 0 7463 0539 7.

How to Get a Job Abroad
Roger Jones BA (Hons) DipEd DPA

The ultimate handbook for all would-be expatriates. 200,000 Britons leave to take jobs abroad each year. How do they do it? Is it luck, or can anyone do it? Written by a former consultant in overseas recruitment, this book explains the qualities, skills and experience you need, and how to identify overseas job opportunities in everything from catering to management and medicine to teaching, tourism or technology. Filled with expert advice, checklists, self-assessment material and extensive reference.

288pp illustrated paperback. 1 85703 003 6. Second edition.